Sean McManus

Cool Scratch
Projects

In easy steps is an imprint of In Easy Steps Limited
16 Hamilton Terrace · Holly Walk · Leamington Spa
Warwickshire · United Kingdom · CV32 4LY
www.ineasysteps.com

In Easy Steps Limited supports The Forest Stewardship Council (FSC),
the leading international forest certification organisation. All our titles
that are printed on Greenpeace approved FSC certified paper carry the
FSC logo.

MIX
Paper from
responsible sources
FSC® C020837

Printed and bound in the United Kingdom

ISBN 978-1-84078-714-6

Contents

Introduction

This book shows you how to build lots of cool projects in Scratch. My other book, Scratch Programming in easy steps, goes into more depth on how Scratch works. Some readers might read that book first and then come here to try these new projects. Others will enjoy making these projects first and then seek out the Scratch Programming book when they want to understand more about what the blocks do.

I recommend you start this book with Magic Mirror and Gribbet!, because they gently introduce some ideas you'll need for other projects later. As you build these projects, think about what each script does, so you avoid making mistakes copying from the book.

Top tips for making these cool projects

 Read the instructions carefully. They'll tell you how to build the scripts and which sprites they belong to.

 Use Scratch 2.0. If you have a choice, use Scratch 2.0. If you're using Scratch 2.0 online, right-clicking doesn't work, so you need to hold the Shift key and click instead.

 Tweak for Raspberry Pi. Look out for special instructions for the Raspberry Pi. Not all projects will work on the Pi, especially if you have an older model.

 Create variables carefully. Check the instructions to see whether the variable is for all sprites or just for one.

Beware of lookalike blocks. Whenever you see a block with **set** or **change** on it, for example, double-check you're using the right one. Look out too for **if** and **if...else**.

Check the details. Make sure you change the menus in the blocks correctly, and type the correct things into the white holes in them.

Take care with yellow brackets. It can get difficult when you have brackets inside brackets, but the program won't work if you put blocks in the wrong place.

Hot tip

If you share these projects or reuse bits of them in your own projects, please mention this book. Thank you!

Beware

Check the first page of each project for any warnings about which computers and Scratch versions the project works on. 3D Artist doesn't work on the Raspberry Pi, for example, and some projects run slowly on the Model B+.

Don't forget

In this book, I've assumed that if you're using Scratch 1.4, you're on a Raspberry Pi, and that if you're using Scratch 2.0, you're using it online.

Visit the author's website for any updates plus bonus content including 10-block demos, videos of these projects, sounds you can use in your games, and more.

Notes and Resources

Downloading the projects

If you can't get the projects to work, or if you want to take a shortcut, you can download the scripts or the images. The examples for Scratch 1.4 on Raspberry Pi can be downloaded from the author's website at **www.sean.co.uk** and the publisher's website at **www.ineasysteps.com** (select the menu entitled Free Resources and choose the Downloads section). The examples for Scratch 2.0 are online at **http://scratch.mit.edu/users/seanmcmanus/**

Installing sounds on the Raspberry Pi

The instruments and drum sounds aren't installed in Scratch on the Raspberry Pi. You'll need them for several projects in this book, including Drum Machine and Gribbet!. To install them:

 In the Pi desktop, click the **Terminal** button at the top. It looks like a computer screen.

 Type the command **sudo apt-get update** in the terminal window.

 Type in **/usr/share/scratch/timidityinstall.sh**

 Type **sudo reboot** in the terminal to reboot your Raspberry Pi. Make sure you've saved all your work first.

Acknowledgements

Thank you to Sevanti and the team at In Easy Steps, David Burder from 3D Images Ltd, Danny Wolfers, and Tim Rowledge. Scratch is developed by the Lifelong Kindergarten Group at the MIT Media Lab. See **http://scratch.mit.edu** ScratchJr is a project of Tufts University, MIT Media Lab, and Playful Invention Company. See **http://scratchjr.org**

Dedication

This book is dedicated to Karen and Leo. Leo loves the color green. We hope he will one day enjoy the inside of this book as much as the cover. Special thanks to Karen for all of her support.

About the author

Sean McManus is an expert technology author. His previous books include Scratch Programming in easy steps, Web Design in easy steps and Raspberry Pi For Dummies (co-authored).

By the same author, **Scratch Programming in easy steps** covers the full range of Scratch's capabilities, and has more detail on how the language works.

1 Magic Mirror

Introducing Magic Mirror

At the funfair, you sometimes see an attraction where your reflection is twisted, stretched and squashed in warped mirrors. Now you can bring the fun home, with the Scratch Magic Mirror. It takes up less space than a funfair, and has three buttons to change the distortion. (Even more magically, it shows the side of you that's facing away from the mirror, although that is more to do with how it works, than anything mystical.)

This project provides an easy start in Scratch, but even if you're an experienced Scratcher, I recommend you try it. Many of the ideas and techniques here will come up again later in this book, and this chapter provides a useful introduction to them.

By making Magic Mirror, you'll discover how to:

- Add sprites and sounds to your project
- Change the background
- Create scripts to control your sprites
- Make sprites move under your control
- Use broadcasts to coordinate between sprites
- Use the graphic effects
- Edit the images used for sprites and backgrounds

Hot tip

The Scripts Area expands to fill the screen space available, so if you use a larger monitor, the Scripts Area will be bigger than in my screenshots.

Hot tip

This script and many others in this book run noticeably faster on the Raspberry Pi if you go into full screen mode. Click the Easel icon, above the Stop button. The Stop button is above the Stage.

Using Scratch

The main parts of the screen in Scratch are:

- **Stage:** This is where you can see your animations and games in action. When Scratch starts, there's a large orange cat in the middle of the Stage.

- **Sprite List:** The cat is a 'sprite', which is like a character or object in a game. The Sprite List shows all the sprites that are in your project. You click them to switch between them.

- **Blocks Palette:** In Scratch, you give the computer commands using blocks, which are instructions that fit together like jigsaw pieces. The Blocks Palette presents you with all the blocks you can use. When you start Scratch, you can see the Motion blocks, which are color-coded in dark blue, and are used for moving sprites. You can browse a different set of blocks in the Blocks Palette by clicking one of the buttons above it, such as the **Looks** button or the **Sound** button.

- **Scripts Area:** The Scripts Area is where you make your programs in Scratch, by joining blocks together there.

The screen is laid out differently in Scratch 1.4 (the older version, but still used on the Raspberry Pi) and Scratch 2.0 (the newer version). See below for the layout in Scratch 2.0, and see page 12 for Scratch 1.4.

Hot tip

There's also ScratchJr for tablet devices, covered in Chapter 11. It's completely different to the computer versions of Scratch.

Hot tip

If you have a choice, pick Scratch 2.0. It doesn't work on the Raspberry Pi or on the iPad, but it runs on most other computers.

11

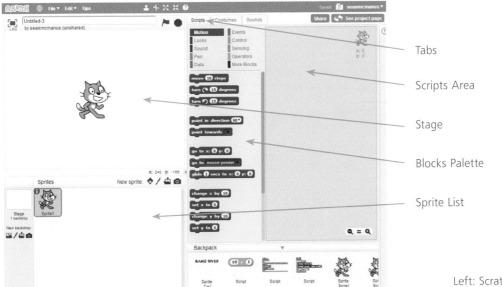

Tabs

Scripts Area

Stage

Blocks Palette

Sprite List

Left: Scratch 2.0

Using Scratch 1.4

The screen layout in Scratch 1.4 is different to Scratch 2.0, and there are two other important differences to look out for:

If you're using Scratch on the Raspberry Pi, you're using Scratch 1.4.

- **See brown, think yellow!**
  There are no Events blocks in Scratch 1.4, but most of them are still there as yellow Control blocks. In this book, when you see a brown block, pretend it's yellow and you'll do fine. Here's the **when green flag clicked** block in Scratch 1.4 (top) and Scratch 2.0 (bottom).

- **Don't get in a spin looking for rotation!**
  Scratch 2.0 has a block called **set rotation style**. This block doesn't exist in Scratch 1.4. Instead, you look above the Blocks Palette and click one of the three buttons to the left of your sprite. The middle button sets the style to left-right.

Scratch 2.0 also has new blocks for cloning sprites and creating your own blocks. I haven't used them in this book, though, so the programs work in Scratch 1.4.

12

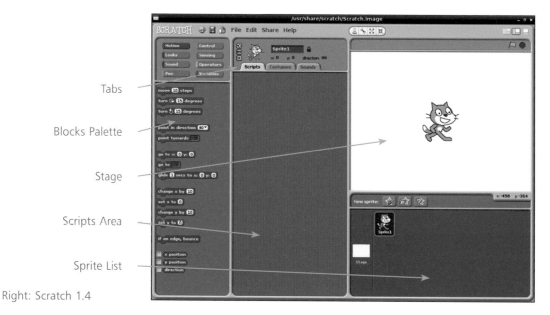

Tabs

Blocks Palette

Stage

Scripts Area

Sprite List

Right: Scratch 1.4

Making the cat move

We'll build up the Magic Mirror program gradually. We'll start with the cat's movement.

1 To start using Scratch on Raspberry Pi, open the Programs Menu and select it in the Programming section. To start using Scratch 2.0 online visit **http://scratch.mit. edu/** in your browser and click **Create** at the top.

2 Click the **Events** or **Control** button above the Blocks Palette. Find the block called **when space key pressed**. Drag it and drop it in the Scripts Area.

3 Click the menu in the block and choose the right arrow key (pictured, right).

4 Click the **Motion** button above the Blocks Palette.

5 Drag a **point in direction 90** block into the Scripts Area. Drop it just underneath your previous block, so that it joins to the previous block. Joined blocks make up what is called a "script". A game is made up of lots of scripts.

6 Drag a **move 10 steps** block in and join it to your script.

7 Click the **Looks** button above the Blocks Palette.

8 Drag a **next costume** block and attach it to the bottom of your script. Check your script with the picture here.

Hot tip

Blocks often have menus, shown with a small triangle pointing down. If you can't find the exact block you need, check for something similar with a menu in it. It might have the option you're looking for.

Don't forget

To get rid of a block again, drag it back into the Blocks Palette. Careful, though: it will take any attached blocks with it!

13

Hot tip

In Scratch 2.0, if you create an account and log in before you start, it will automatically save your work for you. Click your name in the top right to find your projects (or "stuff" as the menu says).

...cont'd

A costume is an image that a sprite has. The cat has two costumes with its legs in different positions. When you switch between them, it looks like its legs are moving. To see the costumes, click the Costumes tab. Click the Scripts tab to get back to the Scripts Area again afterwards.

9 Press the right arrow key on the keyboard, and you should see the cat on the Stage move to the right. The script you've made provides all the instructions for this. It works like a to-do list for the computer, read from top to bottom: "when the right arrow key is pressed, turn to face right, walk ten steps, and then change the costume".

10 Let's add controls to move left. The quickest way to do this is to copy the script we've made and change it. If you're using Scratch 2.0 online, hold down the Shift key and click the script. If you're using Scratch 1.4 or Scratch 2.0 offline, right-click the script. When the menu appears, click **duplicate**. The copied script follows your mouse. Find a blank space in the Scripts Area and click the left mouse button to drop the script there.

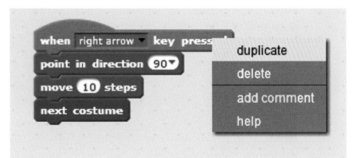

The cat only moves once for each keypress because the **move 10 steps** block moves the cat a distance of 10 steps in one go. It doesn't move the cat 10 times. Try clicking the box in the block and changing the number to see how it affects the cat's movements.

11 In your copied script, click the menus in the **when right arrow key pressed** and **point in direction 90** blocks and change them for the left movement as shown here.

12 What happens when you test it? The cat flips on its head to walk left, because it's been rotated. Let's fix that, and also put the cat in its starting position. See if you

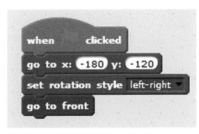

can make the script here. The color of the blocks tells you which part of the Blocks Palette they're in. For blocks with numbers in, you can click the numbers to edit them, delete them or type new numbers in. In Scratch 1.4, there is no **set rotation style** block, so ignore that.

Hot tip

The **go to front** block will make sure the cat appears in front of other sprites in this project, including the mirror and its reflection.

13 In Scratch 1.4, you need to set the rotation style to left-right using a button beside the sprite above the Blocks Palette. It's the middle button with a double-headed arrow on it. Click it to set the rotation style.

Hot tip

When you drag a block out of a script, all the blocks underneath go with it. To remove just one block, first drag it out, with the attached blocks. Then drag the attached blocks away and back into the script. To delete the spare blocks, drag them back into the Blocks Palette.

14 Add the script below to make the cat jump when you press the up arrow key.

Don't forget

The brown Events blocks are yellow Control blocks in Scratch 1.4.

15

Making the mirror

The Stage is looking a bit plain. Let's decorate it.

Scratch 2.0 calls them "backdrops" and Scratch 1.4 calls them "backgrounds". Whatever you call them, they're the images at the back of the Stage. Sprites cannot go behind them.

1 To the left of the Sprite List there is an icon for the Stage. In Scratch 2.0, there is a button underneath it to choose a new backdrop from the library. It looks like a mountain scene (see picture). In Scratch 1.4, click the Stage icon, click the **Backgrounds** tab above the Scripts Area, then click the **Import** button.

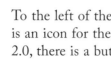

2 In Scratch 2.0, click the Indoors category on the left. In Scratch 1.4, double-click the Indoors folder. You can scroll to see more pictures here. Find a picture you like, click it and then click **OK**.

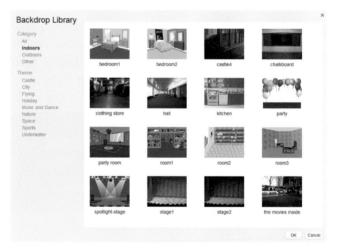

If you make a mistake using the Paint Editor, click the Undo button. In Scratch 2.0, it's an arrow curved to the left, above the canvas. In Scratch 1.4, it says Undo on it, and it's above the Paintbrush tool.

3 The mirror and the wall it hangs on will be another sprite, even though it'll fill the Stage and look like a background. Click the button above the Sprite List to paint a new sprite. The button has a paintbrush on it.

4 In Scratch 1.4, click the magnifying glass with a minus on it to make sure you can see the whole sprite. There should be no scroll bars below or to the right of the canvas.

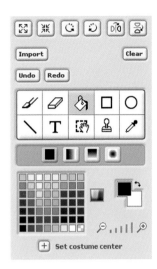

5   Your color palette is underneath the canvas (the drawing area) in Scratch 2.0, and to the left in Scratch 1.4. Click the color you'd like to use for your wall. I chose lilac.

6   The tools are to the left of the canvas area. Click the Fill tool. Click the canvas to fill it with your chosen color.

7   Click the Square/Rectangle tool. The buttons underneath the tools are used to switch between drawing a filled or hollow shape. In Scratch 2.0 (top right) it looks like an unimpressed robot. The buttons for Scratch 1.4 are shown underneath (right, below). Click the solid rectangle option.

Above: The tools panel and color palette in Scratch 1.4. They appear to the left of the canvas. The Fill tool (in blue) is selected in the toolbox. The Rectangle is to its right. The Paintbrush is on the left end of that row of tools.

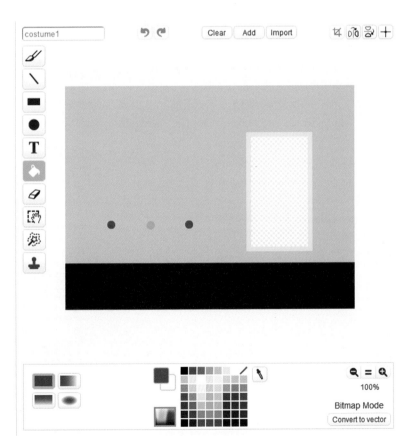

Left: The Paint Editor in Scratch 2.0. The tools are shown on the left. The color palette, fill options and line options appear underneath the canvas.

17

...cont'd

Don't forget

Always make sure you're adding your scripts to the right sprite. Click the sprite in the Sprite List before adding a script to be sure.

Hot tip

Wherever the canvas shows a checked pattern, the images behind the sprite will be visible.

Below: Your images in place. The background shows through the transparent ink in the mirror.

8 Pick a color for the carpet and use the Rectangle tool to draw it. To draw a rectangle, click in the top left corner of your shape, hold down the mouse button and drag to the bottom right. Refer to the picture on page 17 to get an idea of how big to make it, and where to put the mirror and buttons later.

9 We need to change how thick the mirror's frame is, by changing the size of the brush used to draw it. In Scratch 2.0, move the slider underneath the Fill options to the right to make the line thicker. In Scratch 1.4, click the Paintbrush tool, then click the brush size menu under the tools to change the line width. Click the Rectangle tool and select the hollow rectangle option. Pick the frame color for your mirror in the color palette and draw the mirror's frame on the canvas.

10 Pick the transparent ink. In Scratch 2.0, it is in the top right of the color palette and it looks like a red diagonal line. In Scratch 1.4, it's in the bottom right and looks like a checked pattern. Pick the Fill tool and click inside your frame to fill the frame with the transparent ink.

11 Pick the Paintbrush tool. Just click in three places, slightly above the floor, to add three dots. Pick a different color for each one that isn't anywhere else in your image (including the background).

12 In Scratch 1.4, click the **OK** button. In either version, click the **Scripts** tab and add the script on the right to the mirror sprite.

13 Click the **green flag** above the Stage to run this script. It puts the mirror into position, and you should see the background through it.

Adding the reflection

To make the reflection, we'll use a copy of the cat sprite. It is positioned behind the wall, and can only be seen through the transparent ink of the mirror.

1 To start, we'll make a copy of the cat sprite, which will include all its scripts. Shift + click or right-click the cat sprite in the Sprite List. If you're using Scratch 2.0 online, the right-click menu doesn't work, so you have to hold down the Shift key and click instead. In Scratch 1.4 or the offline  version of Scratch 2.0, you can simply right-click. When the menu opens, click **duplicate**.

Below: The information pane in Scratch 2.0

2 Now we have two identical sprites in the project. This could get confusing so let's rename one of them. In Scratch 2.0, click the **i** button on the sprite in the Sprite List and the sprite's name is shown at the top of the information pane that opens. In Scratch 1.4, click the sprite in the Sprite List and its name is shown in a dark box above the Scripts Area. In either case, click the name to edit it, and change the new sprite's name to "reflection". In Scratch 2.0, click the **back** button (right) in the top left of the information pane to go back when you've finished.

3 Click your reflection sprite in the Sprite List. You need to edit the green flag script. Change the numbers in the **go to x: y:** block to -160 and -20 so the reflection appears above and to the left of your main sprite. Add blocks to **go back 2 layers** and **clear graphic effects** at the end.

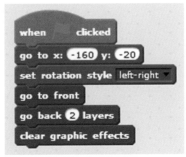

Below: Try it! Click the green flag and move the cat to the mirror.

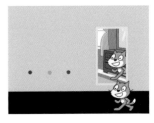

Beware

It's getting confusing now with two cats! Make sure you're adding these scripts to your original Sprite1 cat.

Beware

In Scratch 2.0 on the Sounds tab, there are big speaker icons too, which you should ignore.

Hot tip

Sounds can only be played by a sprite they've been added to. If you can't find a sound effect in the **play sound** block, check you've added it to that sprite.

Adding the magic controls

Now the mirror's working, we can add the magic controls.

 1 Click your original Sprite1 cat in the Sprite List.

2 Click the **Sounds** tab. In Scratch 2.0, click the tiny speaker icon to add a new sound. In Scratch 1.4, click the **Import** button. Go into the Vocals folder and choose the Singer2 sound.

3 Click the **Scripts** tab and find the script that starts with **when green flag clicked**. Add the rest of the blocks shown in this script, starting with the **forever** block. Inside the **forever** block is an **if** block (not an **if... else** block). Inside the **if** block are the **broadcast** and **play sound** blocks. Take care to get the right blocks inside the right brackets. For the **touching color** Sensing block, click the color in it and then click one of the buttons you painted on the wall sprite on the Stage. Broadcasts enable one sprite to send a hidden message to another. The **broadcast** block (which is a yellow Control block in Scratch 1.4) has a menu in it. Click the menu and choose **new message** and create the message with the name of the button color. The **play sound** block also has a menu on it, which you use to choose the Singer2 effect.

```
when      clicked
go to x: -180 y: -120
set rotation style left-right ▼
go to front
forever
    if     touching color ■ ? then
        broadcast red ▼
        play sound singer2 ▼
```

4 If you're using Scratch 2.0 online, hold down the Shift key and click the **if** block in your script. If you're using Scratch 1.4 or Scratch 2.0 offline, right-click the block. When the menu appears, click **duplicate**. Drop your duplicated script underneath your **if** block but inside the **forever** bracket. Change the **touching color** block and the broadcast message for another button, and repeat to set up all three buttons.

Hot tip

If the buttons are too high for the cat to reach, the easiest fix is to edit the wall and mirror image to move the buttons down. Alternatively, you can change the starting y position in the **go to x: y:** block in the **when green flag clicked** scripts on the cat and reflection sprites. Make it a higher number (for example -100 instead of -120) to move the cat up.

21

5 The **broadcast** block is sending a message from the main cat when you jump into one of the buttons. We need to make the reflection cat respond to it. Click the reflection cat in the Sprite List, and add the following scripts. When the reflection receives a broadcast, it will change its appearance using one of the graphics effects.

Beware

The **touching color** block will respond if the cat touches the color, wherever it is. Don't use colors for your buttons that the cat can walk into somewhere else on screen.

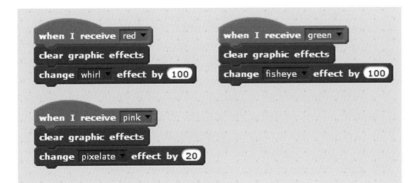

You can share your projects on the Scratch website so people all over the world can enjoy them. Please give credit to this book if you're sharing or adapting its projects. Thank you!

22

Hot tip

Make sure you save your work frequently so you don't lose it. Scratch 2.0 online will save work for you automatically from time to time. In Scratch 1.4, use the File menu.

Below: The color effect can turn the cat green.

Polishing the magic mirror

Congratulations! You've completed the first project in this book. Now you can move the cat using the left, right and up arrow keys. If you jump into a button, it will change the mirror's distortion setting, which you'll see next time you walk in front of it.

The best way to use this book is not just to make the projects, but also see if you can find ways to adapt them, personalize them and improve them. Start by reading the scripts to see if you can work out what they do, and how they work together.

Here are some suggestions for changes you could make:

- **Get arty.** Give the reflection a hat or change its color by editing the costume for the reflection sprite. You could also edit the costume for the wall and mirror sprite to draw some furniture in the room, or a tasteful portrait on the wall.

- **More magic.** You could add more buttons with different graphics effects. If you're a more experienced Scratcher, perhaps you could try adding new costumes to the reflection so that the cat can appear as a dragon in the mirror sometimes. Perhaps you could add a reset button too, to turn the mirror's distortion off?

- **More exercise.** The jump control uses a **repeat 10** block to move the cat up in small steps, and then move it back down again. It's a simple but effective animation. Try experimenting with the numbers in this script. Can you make the cat jump higher, or faster? Can you make the cat furiously kick its legs as it falls through the air after a jump? You'll need a **next costume** block but you'll have to figure out where to put it. You could add different key controls for different styles of jumps.

- **More rooms.** Could you add additional rooms with magic mirrors in? Design the different room walls as costumes in the wall and mirror sprite. Use the **if** block to detect when the cat's x position is more than 230 (leaving on the right), and then change its x position to be on the left (-230 which would be the position arriving on the left). Use a broadcast to get the mirror to change to the next costume too. Can you enable the cat to walk to rooms on the left too? That's a lot harder, because there's no previous costume block.

2 Gribbet!

In this chapter, you'll build the game Gribbet!, which will test your memory as you conduct a choir of frogs. You'll also learn how to use the Paint Editor to make the cartoon sprites.

Introducing Gribbet!

In this chapter, you'll build Gribbet!, a game where you conduct a chorus of friendly frogs.

Here's how you play it: The frogs sing a sequence of notes, and when it's your turn you click the frogs in the same order to play the song back to them. Each time you succeed, another note is added to the song. The frogs always sing the full song so far, before it's your turn to conduct them to play it again. At the top of the screen, you can see whose turn it is, and your score.

At first, the song is just one note long, but with a new note added each round, you'll find your memory is tested as the song gets longer. Each game is unique, with a song randomly created each time you play.

The project is built around some animated frog sprites, which you'll create using the Paint Editor. The frogs look at the singing frog, blink, and follow your mouse pointer with their eyes. Their mouths move when they're singing, and look downcast when the game ends. At the end of each round, the last frog to sing displays a random congratulations message before going into the next round. Small touches like these make the frogs into fun cartoon characters that seem to interact with the player.

At the end of the chapter, there are some suggestions for how you can customize this game and build on the ideas in this project.

Hot tip

As with any game that involves clicking sprites, this is best played in full screen mode. Otherwise, if you slip with the mouse, Scratch will think you're trying to move a sprite on the Stage. To go into full screen mode, click the icon above the Stage. In Scratch 2.0, it's a square icon in the top left. In Scratch 1.4, it's an easel in the top right.

Beware

To get the instruments working on the Raspberry Pi, you need to install them first. See Notes and Resources at the start of this book.

Drawing the frog's body

We'll use the built-in shapes in the Paint Editor to make our frog.

1 Start a new Scratch project and click the paintbrush icon above the Sprite List to paint a new sprite.

2 In **Scratch 1.4**, click the magnifying glass with a minus on it to make sure you can see the whole canvas. You'll need a lot of space to draw the parts for this sprite.

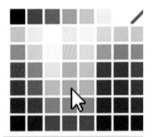

3 In the ink palette, there are several shades of green. Ignore the top two rows of hazy inks. Pick the second solid green ink. We'll use it to draw the body, so we can use a lighter and darker ink for details later.

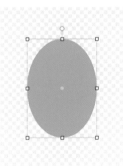

4 Click the circle icon for the Ellipse tool. Click the solid circle shape underneath the tools panel so you're drawing a solid shape, not a hollow one.

5 Click the canvas and hold the mouse button down. Drag down and to the right to draw an ellipse, like an egg balanced upright (see picture, right).

6 Draw another ellipse, this time the other way around. Plant it on top of your first ellipse. These shapes together will be the head and body for your frog sprite.

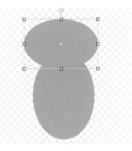

Don't forget

If you hover the mouse pointer over a button, a tip will pop up to tell you what it does. Use this to help you find the right buttons.

Hot tip

In Scratch 2.0, you can click and drag a shape immediately after drawing it. In Scratch 1.4, you can use the Select tool to draw a box around a shape and then drag it into position.

Don't forget

Remember to save your work regularly when working on projects like this.

...cont'd

Make sure you leave plenty of space around your frog's body parts when drawing them. Otherwise, when you come to move them into position, you'll find you're dragging other bits of frog along too.

7 Find an empty space on the canvas and draw a tall, thin ellipse. This will be the frog's leg and we'll rotate it shortly.

8 In **Scratch 2.0**, immediately after drawing the shape, there is a round rotation button above it. Click and hold it, and move the mouse to turn the leg so it points at an angle of about 45 degrees (see top right).

9 In **Scratch 1.4**, after drawing the leg, click the Select tool. Click on the canvas and draw a selection box around the leg. Click the clockwise rotation button (the second button pictured here) once. It's in the top left of the Paint Editor.

10 In **Scratch 2.0**, click the Stamp tool. Draw a selection box around the leg, and drag it to the other side of the frog. The tool will make a copy of the leg for you. Click the **flip left right** button in the top-right of the Paint Editor to make the leg turn the other way.

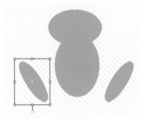

Below: This picture shows your frog so far.

11 In **Scratch 1.4**, click the Stamp tool. Draw a selection box around the leg, and a copy of it follows your mouse cursor. Click on the other side of the frog to stamp a copy there. Click the Select tool and draw a box around the new leg. Click the **flip left-right** button in the top row of the Paint Editor to point the leg the other way.

12 Add some small ellipses for the feet (see picture, right). You'll need to repeat the process you used to draw the leg: draw an ellipse, rotate it, copy it and flip it.

Beware

Once the frog parts are in place, you can't separate them again.

13 Click the Select tool. Draw a selection box around one of the legs and then click and drag it into position. Repeat the process to position the foot, and then put the other limb and foot into place too (see second picture, right).

Hot tip

To copy a costume in Scratch 2.0, Shift + click it in the Costumes Area and then choose **duplicate**. In Scratch 1.4, click the Copy button beside it in the Costumes Area.

14 Pick a darker green from the palette and draw an ellipse in the middle of the frog's body (see third picture, right).

15 Pick the lighter solid green from the palette. Click the Paintbrush tool and set the paintbrush size to about three quarters of the maximum. Draw two lines for the frog's arms. Use a slightly bigger pen to plot a circle at the end of the arms for the hand. Then use a smaller pen to draw the fingers. I also used a slightly bigger pen to plot pads at the ends of the fingers.

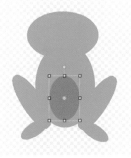

Below: The frog body in its finished form.

16 The body is now finished.
Make two copies of the costume, so you end up with one frog sprite with three identical body costumes.

Hot tip

We could have put the nostrils onto the body costume and copied them across all three mouth costumes to get them in exactly the same place for each costume. But it looks cute if the nose twitches a little bit when the mouth moves.

Hot tip

To test the animation, click the different costumes in the Costumes Area and watch the sprite change on the Stage.

Drawing the frog's face

Each of the three costumes will be used for a different mouth position: happy, sad and singing.

1 Rename your first costume to "happy". In **Scratch 2.0** (pictured, right), you can change its name above the tools in the Paint Editor.
In **Scratch 1.4**, edit its name in the dark box beside its image in the Costumes Area. In Scratch 1.4, click the **Edit** button to edit the costume.

2 Adjust the paintbrush size so it's not too thick. We're about to draw the mouth. Click the Ellipse tool and the black ink. Click the shape underneath the tools to choose the hollow ellipse.

3 Find an empty space on the image and draw an ellipse. If you put it beside the head, you can estimate the right size.

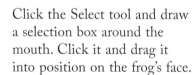

4 Click the Eraser tool and use it to delete the top half-and-a-bit of the ellipse.

5 Click the Paintbrush tool and use it to draw two small lines at each end of the mouth.

6 Click the Select tool and draw a selection box around the mouth. Click it and drag it into position on the frog's face.

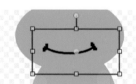

7 Use the Paintbrush to draw two nostrils a little bit above the mouth. In Scratch 1.4, click **OK** to finish.

8 Now we'll repeat that process, with a few changes, to draw the other mouth positions. Rename the second costume to "sad" and click the **Edit** button in Scratch 1.4.

9 For the sad mouth, you use a much smaller ellipse, and delete more of it to leave a shorter line. Don't add the paintbrush lines this time. Try to get the nostrils roughly the same distance apart, but it's okay if they are in a slightly different position to the previous costume.

10 Rename the third costume to "singing". For this one, use the Ellipse tool to make a solid black circle. Draw a solid red ellipse inside it for the frog's tongue.

11 Click the Paintbrush button above the Sprite List to draw a new sprite (not a new costume). This is for the eye.

12 Draw a solid white circle. Inside the white circle, draw a small black circle for the pupil of the eye. It should be facing to the right.

13 Copy the eye costume, and edit the new costume. Fill both circles with dark green and use the Paintbrush to clean up any remaining black or white. This will be the closed eye. You should end up with one eye sprite with two costumes: eye open, and eye shut.

14 Rename your eye costumes to "eye open" and "eye shut".

Hot tip

Putting the eyes in a different sprite enables us to move them independently of the mouth.

Don't forget

When you draw a new sprite in Scratch, you always draw it in its "facing right" position.

Hot tip

The eyes will bulge out of the top of the frog's head, so you can make them quite large.

Drawing the background

We'll use the cat sprite to coordinate the game, and draw the background. Let's add the background now. It'll make it easier for us to position the frogs and their eyes.

1 Click the Stage icon beside the Sprite List. Click the **Backdrops** or **Backgrounds** tab, and in Scratch 1.4, click the **Edit** button. Fill the background with a dark green ink, for the grassy bank of the river.

2 Click the **Scripts** tab and then click the **Data** or **Variables** button above the Blocks Palette and make a new variable. Call it *grass x*. It can be for all sprites.

3 Give the cat this script. You'll need to make a new broadcast for "draw scene". In the second **go to x: y:** block, add the blocks in this order: **go to x: y:, +, *, sin, grass x**. The **sin** block is the **sqrt of 9** block with a different menu option. In the second **go to x: y:** block, add the blocks in this order: **go to x: y:, grass x, +, y position, pick random**.

Hot tip

The **sin** block is a mathematical function called Sine. Using it, you can draw curves, as we have for the river bank here.

Don't forget

The colors of the blocks tell you where to find them in the Blocks Palette. For example, the hide block is purple, so click the purple Looks button above the Blocks Palette to find it. The only exception is that brown blocks are yellow in Scratch 1.4.

Below: Click the script to see the background drawn, like this.

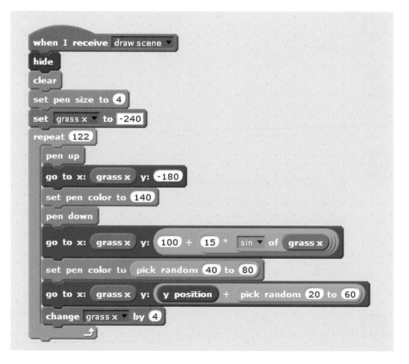

Animating the eyes

Let's add the script to animate the eye. We'll duplicate the eye sprite and its code to make both eyes for all the frogs.

1 Click the **Data** or **Variables** button above the Blocks Palette and make three new variables for all sprites: *singing frog*, *blinking frog*, and *turn*. The *blinking frog* variable is used for which frog number should be blinking. The *turn* variable is used to say whose turn it is to play, and will store "frogs", "player" or "game over".

2 Click the eye sprite in the Sprite List and add this code:

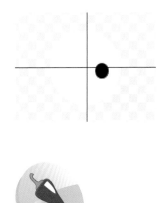

3 Shift + click or right-click the eye sprite in the Sprite List and duplicate it. You can position the eyes on the Stage on top of your frog body.

4 Click the cat sprite in the Sprite List and add these scripts on the right to the cat.

Hot tip

If the eye looks odd when it rolls, edit its costume, click the **Set costume center** button and then click in the middle of the eye. In Scratch 2.0, the button is in the top right.

Hot tip

For *point towards singing frog*, use **point towards mouse-pointer** and add the **singing frog** block on top.

Beware

Don't mix up the **set [variable name] to [number]** and the **change [variable name] by [number]** blocks.

...cont'd

Hot tip

If you find the game doesn't respond to your mouse clicks when you're playing it, it might be because the computer can't cope with all the animation. Add a wait block as recommended in Step 5 to fix that.

Beware

Make sure that the eyes that respond to the same blinking frog number are next to either other. Otherwise, you'll have frogs winking at each other.

Below: A frog and four pairs of floating eyes, eerily following your mouse pointer.

5 On the Raspberry Pi, Scratch can struggle to keep up with ten eyes moving all the time. To solve this, add a **wait 1 secs** block after the **broadcast move eyes and wait** block in the cat's script. This will make the eye movements a bit jerkier, but they're still effective.

6 Click the **Data** or **Variables** button above the Blocks Palette. Find the **set variable name to 0** block. Click the menu in the block to change

the variable to turn. Edit the value in the block, changing it from 0 to player. Click the block. If you tick the box beside the variable name you can confirm on the Stage that the variable now contains "player".

7 Click the **green flag** and move your mouse around the Stage. You should see the eyes look towards your mouse pointer, as you move it around. If you wait long enough, the eyes will eventually blink.

8 Shift + click or right-click your eye in the Sprite List and duplicate it twice. Drag the two new eyes away from your original pair on the Stage.

9 Click one of the new eyes in the Sprite List and edit its script. Change the number in the **if blinking frog = 1** block to 2 (as shown below). Repeat this for the other eye.

10 Repeat the duplication and editing until you have five pairs of eyes responding to blinking frog numbers 1, 2, 3, 4, and 5.

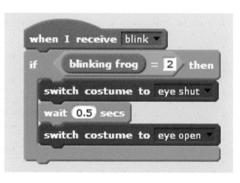

Setting up the variables

Let's set up the additional variables the game needs.

1 Click the **Data** or **Variables** button. Make new variables for all sprites called *score*, *somebody's singing*, *title*, *counter*, and *notes played*. Create new lists called *scale*, *sequence* and *round messages*. The *scale* contains the notes the frogs sing. The *sequence* is the song that gets longer with each round played. One of the *round messages* is shown at the end of each round.

2 Click the cat in the Sprite List and add the script below to it. Click the script to run it.

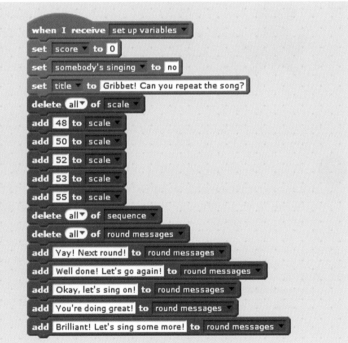

3 In the Blocks Palette, go into the Data or Variables section. Clear the boxes beside all the variables and lists, except for title, turn and score. Drag those boxes on the Stage to arrange them at the top as shown below.

Hot tip

The variable *somebody's singing* is used to store whether a frog is singing now or not. We use it to stop the player setting two frogs singing at the same time.

Hot tip

If you don't see the message you need in the menu of a **broadcast** or **when I receive** block, create a new message for it.

Hot tip

When you make a variable or list, it's usually a good idea to hide it from the Stage. To do that, clear the box beside its name in the Blocks Palette.

Gribbet! Can you repeat the song?   player   0

Adding the frogs' scripts

The next step is to add the scripts to our frog body.

Hot tip

When you make the variable *this frog*, clear the box beside its name in the Blocks Palette.

1 Rename your frog body sprite to "Frog 1". To rename a sprite in Scratch 2.0 (pictured below), click the **i** button on the sprite in the Sprite List and then type the new name into the text box at the top of the pane. Click the back button on the left when you've finished. In Scratch 1.4, click the sprite in the Sprite List, and then click and edit the name in the dark box above the Scripts Area, beside the sprite image.

Back button

Beware

It's really important to make the variable *this frog* for this sprite only. Making a variable for one sprite enables us to have variables with the same name on different sprites, so we can reuse our scripts more easily. All our frogs will have a variable called *this frog* but they will store a different number in it so they can sing different notes and work out whether the player is playing the right notes.

2 Make a new variable called *this frog*. Select the option to make this variable **for this sprite only**. Clear the box beside it in the Blocks Palette to hide it from the Stage.

New Variable
Variable name: this frog
○ For all sprites   ● For this sprite only
OK   Cancel

3 Add the code shown on the right to your frog body sprite.

4 Add the script on the right to your frog. You can click it to see the frog's expression go sad, and then click the other script on your frog to cheer it up again.

In the **join Frog this frog** block, put a single space after "Frog". We'll combine that word with the variable number to get the sprite names "Frog 1", "Frog 2" and so on. Without the space, it won't work.

5 Add the script below to your frog. Click it to see and hear your frog sing its note. If you're using Scratch 1.4, the instrument numbers are different. Try numbers 53, 54 or 55 for a choir sound.

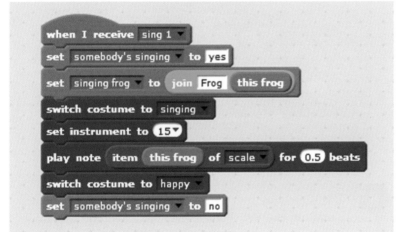

You'll need to make a new message for "sing 1" in the **when I receive** block.

6 Add the script below to your frog sprite. In Scratch 1.4, the **item random of [list name]** block is called **item any of [list name]**.

When you use the **item 1 of [list name] block**, you usually need to change the item number and the list name.

...cont'd

Be careful with the brackets here. You have an **if...then** bracket, with an **if...then...else** bracket inside it. Make sure the other blocks go inside the right brackets.

Hot tip

The **when this sprite clicked** block will be called **when Frog 1 clicked** in Scratch 1.4. The name of the sprite in it changes to whichever sprite the block is on.

Don't forget

The **if...then...else** block is called **if...else** in Scratch 1.4. The **if...then** block is called **if**.

7 We'll now build the final script we need to add to the frog body. Start by putting an **if...then...else** block inside an **if...then** block. In the diamond hole of the outer **if** block, add the blocks in this order: **and**, **=**, **=**, **turn**, **somebody's singing**. In the **if...then...else** block, add the blocks in this order: **=**, **item 1 of [list name]**, **+**, **this frog**, **notes played**. Remember to change the list to the right name in the block here.

```
when this sprite clicked
if < turn = player > and < somebody's singing = no > then
    if < this frog = item (notes played + 1) of sequence > then
        change notes played ▼ by 1
        change score ▼ by 10
    else
        set turn ▼ to game over
        say Oops!
    broadcast join sing this frog and wait
```

8 Duplicate your frog body sprite four times, so you have a total of four frog bodies. In Scratch 2.0, the new frogs will be correctly named. In Scratch 1.4, rename the new frogs to Frog 2, Frog 3, Frog 4 and Frog 5.

9 In the green flag script of each frog, change the value of the *this frog* variable to 2 for Frog 2 (as shown here), 3 for Frog 3 and so on.

```
when      clicked
set this frog ▼ to 2
switch costume to happy ▼
```

10 For each frog, change the message in the **when I receive sing 1** block to sing 2, sing 3, sing 4 and sing 5, matching the *this frog* values. Make a new message for each one.

Making the final images

Now we have the frog bodies, we can finish our images, including the tick and cross that will be used when the game ends.

1 Click the button above the Sprite List to draw a new sprite. Draw five brown ovals to represent the lily pads that the frogs will sit on. Make sure there's plenty of space around them, especially at the top.

2 Now drag the sprites on the Stage to put the lily pads on the pond, the bodies on the lily pads, and the eyes on the bodies.

3 In **Scratch 2.0**, click the cat sprite in the Sprite List and click the **Costumes** tab. Click the button to choose a costume from the library and add the costume button4-a (a tick) from the Things category. Add another costume, this time button5-b (a red cross). Rename the tick costume to "tick" and the cross costume to "cross". You rename the costume in the white box at the top of the Costumes Area.

4 In **Scratch 1.4**, click the cat sprite in the Sprite List and click the **Costumes tab**. Click the **Paint** button, paint a white tick and click OK. Click the **Paint** button to add another costume, and make this one a big red cross. Rename the costumes in the Costumes Area to "tick" and "cross".

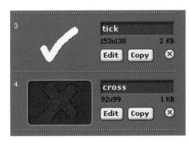

Click the Enlarge or Shrink button at the top of the screen (shown for Scratch 1.4) and then click a sprite on the Stage to adjust its size.

You can match any frog body with any pair of eyes on the Stage.

In Scratch 1.4, I made the tick white so it can be seen clearly on top of the green frogs. The green tick in Scratch 2.0 has a black outline, so this isn't a problem.

Adding the main game script

Everything is in place now for us to add the final game script. Here we go!

1 Click the cat in the Sprite List and add the script on the right to it. This skeleton script helps to get the brackets in the right place.

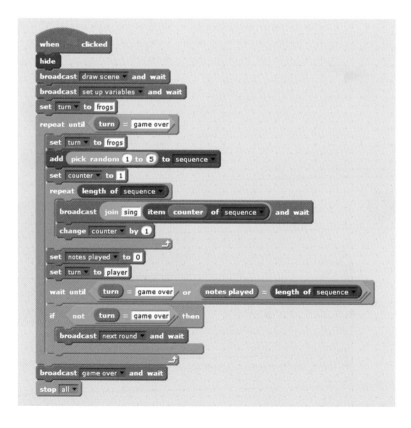

2 Now add the rest of the blocks, as shown below. Add a single space after "sing" in the **join** block. In the **wait until** block,

add the **or** block first, then the two = blocks in each side of it. Take special care with the variable and list blocks to choose the right blocks and menu options.

Ending the game

When the game finishes, the frogs look sad and the player is shown the frog they should have clicked.

 1 Add the following script to the cat sprite.

```
when I receive game over
broadcast sad and wait
pen up
show
go to front
repeat 5
    switch costume to cross
    go to singing frog
    wait 0.5 secs
    switch costume to tick
    go to join Frog item notes played + 1 of sequence
    wait 0.5 secs
broadcast sad
hide
```

The **broadcast and wait block** pauses until all the scripts triggered by the message have finished. It can help ensure that things happen in the right order.

The **go to** block here is the **go to mouse-pointer** or **go to [sprite name]** block. You can drop other blocks on top of it. We're using a simple formula to work out which sprite to go to, the next number in the sequence.

2 Click the script to test it. You should see the frog's faces look glum. A tick will flash on the frog that should have sung, and a cross will flash on the frog the player clicked. Until you've played a game, it'll flash on the same frog.

Click the green flag to play. What's the highest score you can get?

Customizing Gribbet!

You could use the boggly eyes on other characters and animals too. Books for young children often include simplified animal drawings you can use for inspiration. Try visiting a library if you don't have any at home.

There are lots of things you can do to improve and personalize Gribbet! Here are some suggestions to start with:

- **Accessorize!** There are lots of sprites you can use to decorate your frogs. The eyes are set to come to the front when the green flag is clicked, so if you want a sprite in front of the eyes (like glasses), give it this script too.

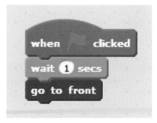

- **Different voices.** You can change the instrument used for each frog to make them sound different. You could use sound effects instead of notes, perhaps even recording your own croaking noises.

- **Body movements.** You could edit the singing costume so the frogs throw their arms up when they sing. The frogs don't all need to look alike, either: you can make each one look unique or move uniquely.

- **Customized messages.** You can give each frog a different message in place of "Oops!". You can add more messages to the round messages list to congratulate the player too.

- **Change the tune.** Can you make the game play a particular tune? This is for more experienced Scratchers!

Right: The frogs with a variety of accessories found in Scratch 2.0.

3 Drum Machine

Introducing Drum Machine

Whether you're a musician or not, everybody enjoys having a go on the drums. With this project, you'll build a drum machine that you can use to make rhythms. It supports 16 beats and 8 different drum sounds, although you could use it to make a sequence of any sound in Scratch 2.0.

It works like this: you see a grid of buttons that you can turn on (blue) or off (white). Each row (or line from left to right) represents a different instrument. So the top row might be a snare drum, and the next row might be a kick drum, for example.

A green beat marker moves along the top of the grid, from left to right. At each step, if a drum's button is on, that drum plays. In the screenshot below, you can see that the snare drum (top row) plays on the 1st beat, 5th beat, 9th beat and 13th beat, because those spots are blue. That's a good backbone for your beat: ONE two three four, ONE two three four...

This project shows how the pen can be used not just for drawing pictures, but also for creating ways to interact with people using your programs. The spots are all drawn by moving 1 step with the pen down. A single list, called *drum settings*, is used to remember whether each button is on or off. The first 16 list entries are for the top row, the next 16 are for the second row, and so on. A simple calculation is used to find the right item in the list when working out whether to play a beat or not.

Hot tip

You can see a short video showing this project and others from the book at www.ineasysteps.com and the author's website: www.sean.co.uk
This is a difficult project to explain, so if you're not sure how it works, take a look at the video.

Don't forget

Brown blocks are yellow Control blocks in Scratch 1.4. You'll see a lot of them in this chapter!

Beware

This project needs the instruments to be installed on the Raspberry Pi. See the Notes at the start of the book. This project runs slower on the Model B+ Raspberry Pi and may slow down when the mouse is moving.

42

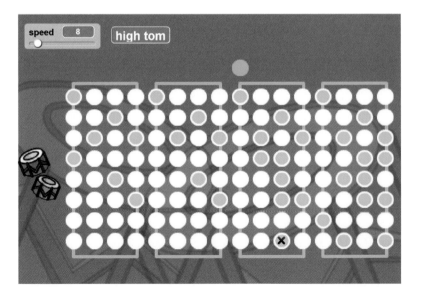

Drawing the background

Let's start by creating the background, which is drawn using some large and faded out drum sprites.

1 Click the Stage beside the Sprite List. Click the **Backdrops** or **Backgrounds** tab, and in Scratch 1.4 click **Paint**. Fill the background with brown ink.

2 Click the button above the Sprite List to add a new sprite from the library in Scratch 2.0, or from a file in Scratch 1.4. Go into the Things folder and add Drum1. Repeat the process to also add Drum2.

3 Click Drum1 in the Sprite List and give it the first script on this page. In Scratch 1.4, only add the first five blocks (finish with **go to x:-220 y:0**).

4 Click Drum2 in the Sprite List. Give it the second script here. In Scratch 1.4, only add the first five blocks.

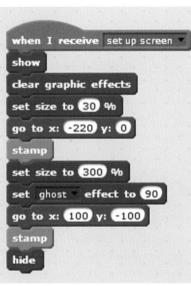

Script 1

Script 2

You can make your program more interesting by using sprites in this way to add some texture to your screen design.

Note the special instructions for Scratch 1.4 (which includes the Raspberry Pi) here! The **stamp** block works differently there so we can't use the faded background drums.

Below: Click both scripts to test them and see the backdrop to Drum Machine. The faded drums only work in Scratch 2.0.

The spots are grouped in blocks of four to make it easier to see the patterns of the rhythm. I put two tiny drums on the left to hint that the rows represented instruments too. When you're designing a project, try to think of ways to make it less confusing for people using it for the first time.

44

Drawing the grid

The cat sprite is the conductor of our drum machine, in charge of the timings and the grid.

1 Click the cat sprite in the Sprite List and add the two scripts here to it. The "set up screen" script is used to draw the four boxes underneath the grid. These are rectangles with matching long and short sides, so a **repeat 2** block is used to draw the two halves (short side, long side) and turn the sprite ready for the next two. There are four boxes, so that process repeats four times, moving across the screen between each box. The second script here draws 8 rows of 16 spots. With both scripts, take care to get the blocks inside and outside the right **repeat** brackets. Remember to click the number in the **repeat 10** block and edit it to the number you need.

Below: The grid appears on top of the background images.

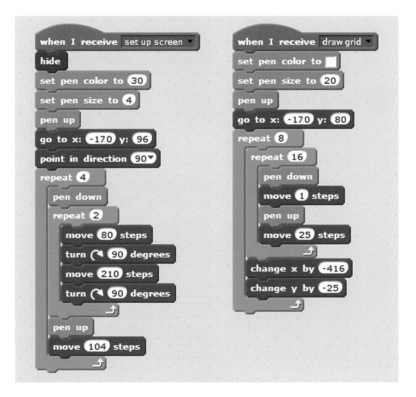

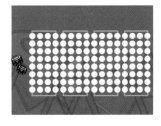

2 Click both scripts to test them; the "set up screen" script first. You should see the grid appear.

Adding the beat marker

The beat marker moves across the top of the grid, indicating which drums are being played at a particular time. The beat marker is managed by the cat.

1 Click the **Data** or **Variables** button and click the button to **Make a Variable**. Create a variable called *beat* for all sprites, and another called *speed*, also for all sprites. The beat variable is used to remember which beat in the pattern the program is up to, from 0 to 15. The speed variable controls how long the marker waits before moving on to the next beat, so it controls how fast the music is.

New Variable
Variable name: beat
● For all sprites   ○ For this sprite only
OK   Cancel

Hot tip

A variable is used to remember information in a program. In Scratch 2.0, you make a variable using the Data part of the Blocks Palette. In Scratch 1.4, you use the Variables section.

2 Click the cat in the Sprite List and add this script to it. In the **wait** block, add the / Operator block (for dividing numbers) and then drop the **speed** block on top. Make new messages for "mark beat", "beat" and "clear beat" in the **broadcast and wait** blocks.

```
when clicked
set speed to 30
clear
broadcast set up screen and wait
broadcast draw grid and wait
forever
    set beat to 0
    repeat 16
        broadcast mark beat and wait
        broadcast beat and wait
        wait speed / 60 secs
        broadcast clear beat and wait
        change beat by 1
```

...cont'd

Our background images have to be below the beat marker, otherwise it will stamp a brown hole in them as it moves across the screen.

3 Add the scripts below to the cat sprite. The "mark beat" script is used to draw the green beat marker. The "clear beat" script is used to delete it before it moves on to its next position. In the "clear beat" script, grab the color in the **set pen color** block from the top of the Stage. The pen size is slightly larger in the deletion script, otherwise there's a ghost of an outline left behind. In theory, it should work with identical pen sizes for stamping and deleting, but in practice it doesn't. It's a quirk of Scratch!

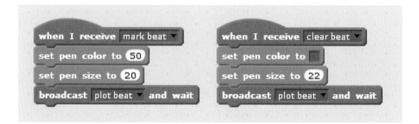

46

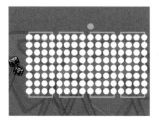

Don't forget

The x position is how far across the screen, from left to right, a sprite is. The y position is how far up or down the screen it is.

4 Add the script below to the cat sprite. In the **go to x: y:** block, add the blocks in this order: **+**, *****, **beat**. The x position is worked out by taking the edge of the grid (-170), and adding 26 times the beat to it. Why 26? Because when we drew the grid, each spot was 1 step, with a gap of 25 steps to the next one. So this calculation lines up the marker with the grid columns below.

```
when I receive plot beat ▼
pen up
go to x: -170 + 26 * beat y: 115
pen down
move 1 steps
```

Below: Click the green flag to see the marker move across the grid.

Adding the cursor

The cursor is used to show the user where they are in the grid as they move around it, turning drums on or off.

1 Add a sprite to use as the cursor. In Scratch 2.0, use the Button5 sprite, which is a black X. In Scratch 1.4, use the beachball sprite. The button to add the sprite is above the Sprite List and both are in the Things folder. In Scratch 2.0, click the button to add a sprite from the library.

2 Click the **Data** or **Variables** button above the Blocks Palette. Make two variables called *user x* and *user y*, both for all sprites. These will remember where the user is in the grid.

3 Add the scripts below to your cursor sprite. In each of the holes in the **go to x: y:** block, add blocks in this order: **+** or **-**, ***** and then the variable block.

Hot tip

Programmers often count from 0, instead of 1. That's what I'm doing for the user x and user y variables. The top left position in the grid is where user x and user y are both 0. It makes the calculations simpler when positioning the cursor because it keeps the start positions consistent with drawing the grid.

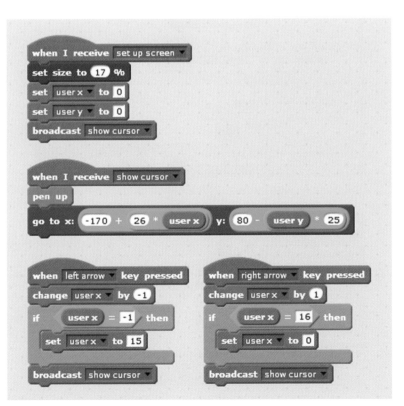

Beware

Don't mix up the user x and user y variables. If the cursor moves in an odd way, check these are right.

Below: The cursor image in Scratch 2.0 (left) and Scratch 1.4 (right).

...cont'd

The wrap around effect works by checking the x position and, if it's too big or too small for the grid, setting it to the final position on the opposite side. It only needs to check for values too small when the left key is pressed, and too big when going right.

4 Click the **green flag** to set up the program. When the grid has been drawn, press the left and right cursor keys to check that your cursor moves along the top row of the grid. It should wrap around, so if you go off the left, it comes back on the right and vice versa.

5 Click the **Data** or **Variables** button above the Blocks Palette. Make a variable called *drum* and a list called *drum names*, both for all sprites.

6 Add the scripts below to your cursor sprite.

7 Test the up and down cursor movement, including wrapping around from top to bottom.

In the "show cursor" script, the x position calculation should look familiar from the beat tracker. The y position is calculated by taking the top edge of the grid and taking off 25 times the user y variable. The gap is 25 because the grid spots are 25 steps apart vertically. You can check this in the script that draws the grid.

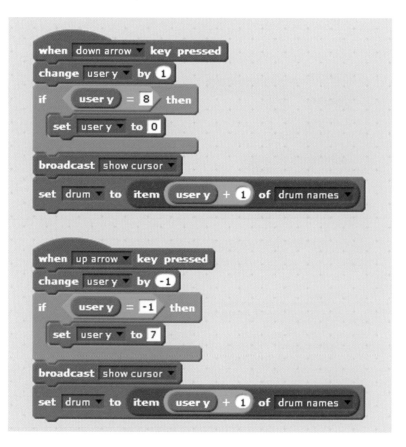

Adding the switch controls

The space bar is used to toggle the switch under the cursor on or off. It changes the appearance in the grid, and also changes the value in the drum settings list. The next step is to add the script that does that.

1 Click the **Data** or **Variables** button above the Blocks Palette. Make a variable called *on or off* for all sprites.

2 Add the script below to your cursor sprite.

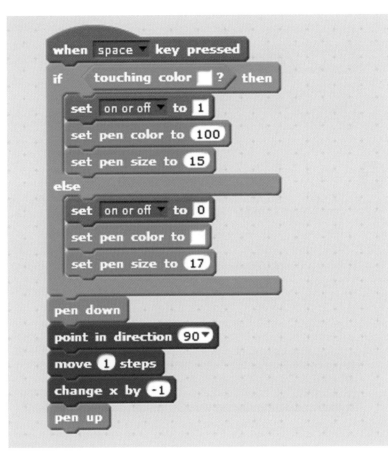

Hot tip

Programs often use 1 to mean "on" and 0 to mean "off". I could have just used the words "on" or "off", but there's less risk of making a mistake using just 0 and 1.

Hot tip

The Stage is probably getting quite cluttered with variables and lists now, so clear the boxes beside them in the Data or Variables section of the Blocks Palette to hide them from the Stage.

3 Click the **green flag** and test the program so far by moving around the grid and tapping the space bar. You should be able to turn the drum buttons on and off again all over the grid.

...cont'd

Hot tip

Try to work out which list item should change and what it should become before you press the space bar. That way you can check the program is working correctly.

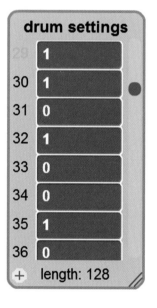

4 Click the **Data** or **Variables** button above the Blocks Palette. Make a variable called *settings number* and a list called *drum settings*, both for all sprites.

5 The *drum settings* list stores whether each drum is on or off. First, we create an empty list. Add the following script to your cursor sprite and click the **green flag** to run it.

6 Add the next script to your cursor. The *settings number* variable is for the item in the list that matches the grid position the cursor is on. It's calculated by multiplying the row (*user y*) by 16 (because each row is 16 spots wide), and adding *user x*. Because our user variables start at 0 but list positions start at 1, we add 1 to the result. Add the blocks in this order: +, + (to the right of the first +), * (to the left of the second +), *user y* and *user x*.

In Step 7, you're going back to a previous script, not adding to the one you just built.

7 Drag these blocks and attach them to the end of the **when space key pressed** script on your cursor sprite.

8 Tick the box beside *drum settings* in the Blocks Palette and turn drums on and off to see how the list changes.

Adding a drum

Now it's time to get musical! Let's add our first drum.

1 Add any sprite to your project to use as the drum.

2 Click the **Data** or **Variables** button and make two variables called *drum number* and *list item number*. Select the option to make them **for this sprite only**.

3 Add the scripts below to your drum sprite. Add the maths Operator blocks in this order: +, +, *.

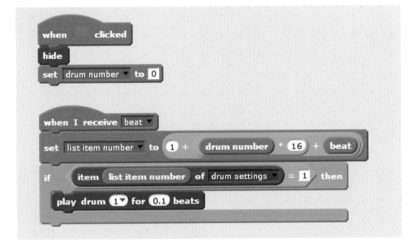

4 In Scratch 2.0, you can use sounds instead of the built-in drums if you like. Click the **Sounds** tab and click the button to add a new sound from the library. Go to the Percussion folder and choose a short sound. You can click the play button to hear a sound before you add it. If you add a sound, replace the **play drum** block in your script above with a **play sound** block for your new sample.

51

...cont'd

5 Click the green flag to start the program and test it works. You should be able to turn on the drums in the top row, and hear them play when the green beat marker reaches them.

6 In Scratch 2.0, Shift + click your drum sprite in the Sprite List. In Scratch 1.4, right-click it. In either version, choose **Duplicate** in the menu when it opens.

7 Click your duplicated sprite in the Sprite List. If you're using recorded sounds, go to the **Sounds** tab and add a new sound to your sprite. Again, make it a short sound.

8 Next, you need to edit the scripts on your duplicated drum sprite. Change the number in the set **drum number to 0** block to be 1. Drum numbers start at 0, so the second drum is number 1 and the third one is number 2 and so on. If you're using sounds, change the **play sound** block so it plays the new sound you added. Otherwise, change the drum number in the **play drum** block to another type of drum.

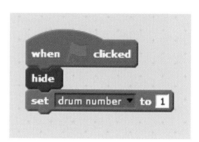

Below: Some of the built-in drum sounds in Scratch 2.0.

9 Repeat this process by duplicating the sprite and adding 1 to the drum number each time. You should end up with eight drum sprites, with a drum number from 0 to 7, and with each one playing a different sound.

10 Test it! Click the **green flag** to start the program. Try turning on all the drums at different times so you can hear them working.

Adding finishing touches

Now for the final finishing touches!

1 Click the **Data** or **Variables** button above the Blocks Palette. Find the blocks for the *drum* and *speed* variables and check or tick the boxes beside them. Clear the boxes for any other variables or lists to tidy up the Stage.

2 On the Stage, double-click the speed box until the slider appears in it. Double-click the drum box until it is empty. Drag the boxes to the top left corner of the Stage, with the speed box on the left.

Hot tip

The slider in the variable box is a handy control that's built in to Scratch. It makes it easy to enable users to change the numbers in variables.

3 Click your cursor sprite in the Sprite List, and find its script that starts with the **when green flag clicked** block Add the new blocks shown below to the script, starting with the **delete all of drum names** block. For the next blocks, add the names of your drum sounds in order of their *drum number*. You might need to click on your drum sprites to check which sound they are playing.

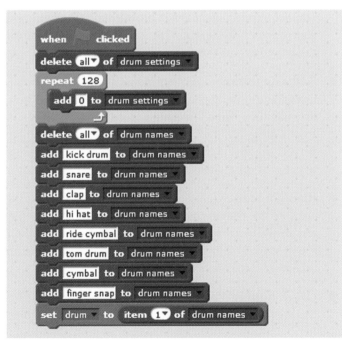

Hot tip

Click the green flag and when the program is ready, try changing the speed using the slider. You should see the beat marker speed up or slow down, and hear your rhythm get faster or slower if you have any drums turned on.

Remixing Drum Machine

Now you've built Drum Machine, there are lots of ways you can adapt it. Here are some suggestions.

- **Record Sounds.** You can record your own sounds to use in this program. In the **Sounds** tab there is a **Record** button, which looks like a microphone in Scratch 2.0. Perhaps you could try beatboxing, making drum sounds with your mouth?

- **Musical sounds.** Drum Machine can be used for any kinds of sounds. You could make each row play a different musical note and use the grid to compose short jingles.

- **Better samples.** There are lots of professional audio samples on the web for musicians that you can download. You will need to download a zip file and extract it. To add the downloaded sounds to a sprite, click the sprite in the Sprite List and go to the **Sounds** tab. In Scratch 2.0, click the folder icon and in Scratch 1.4, click the **Import** button. Use the file browser to find where you saved your samples. In Scratch 1.4 (pictured), use the buttons on the left to get to the desktop or other parts of the computer.

- **Add a metronome.** A metronome is used to keep time in music, and usually plays a high drum on the first beat of a bar, and then three low sounds for the other beats of a bar. In our program, the bars are marked out by the rectangles behind the grid. Can you add a metronome that users can turn on or off to help them when making their rhythms?

- **Random beats.** Can you make the drum machine start with some of the drums turned on for some of the beats, chosen at random? There are a couple of different ways to do this, but it will work best if you don't have too many drums turned on, otherwise it will just sound chaotic.

- **Glitch button.** Can you add a button to make the beat tracker jump back to the start, so the rhythm jumps?

4 12 Angry Aliens

If you have the ebook or the pdf version of this book, to get our 3D glasses, or to purchase extra pairs, visit our website www.ineasysteps.com/cool-scratch-projects-in-easy-steps

This project works but runs slowly on the Raspberry Pi Model B+. I recommend using a more recent model, or using Scratch 2.0 on a PC if possible.

Introducing 12 Angry Aliens

Although this game is inspired by a long line of sci-fi shoot-em-ups, it adds a new dimension: depth. To play this game and see the 3D effect, you'll need the 3D glasses that are included with this book (paperback edition only), or another pair of red and cyan anaglyph glasses.

As the aliens rush towards you, and even appear to pop out of the screen, you're under pressure to shoot them. Each shot costs you 5 points and you get more points the further away the alien is when you hit it. Use the cursor keys to move, and tap space to fire.

As you build this project, you'll learn how the 3D effect works so that you can use it in your own games. The full screen mode makes the game run faster on the Raspberry Pi Model B+, but to use full screen mode you'll need to sit some distance from the screen. You might find the game works best when looking at the normal sized Stage in the script editor. If you can't see the 3D effect at first, take a moment to let your eyes relax and give them time to adjust. If you usually wear glasses, wear the 3D glasses outside your normal glasses. To avoid your eyes getting tired, take regular breaks and only wear the 3D glasses when testing the graphics effects and playing the game.

The 3D effect only works on the screen. The images in this book will help you build the project but they won't work with the glasses. For a 3D preview, visit **www.ineasysteps.com** or the author's website, **www.sean.co.uk**

Because of printing limitations, the 3D effect only works on the screen.

How the 3D effect works

Before we make the game, it's a good idea to understand how the 3D effect works. We can see distances because we have two eyes and they each see a slightly different image of the world. Our brain decodes these images to work out how far away things are. Using anaglyph glasses, we can trick the brain into seeing depth on a flat screen, because the glasses enable us to show each eye a slightly different image.

The glasses have two colored lenses:

- The red lens filters out the red so only the cyan gets through.

- The cyan lens filters out the cyan color, so only the red gets through.

For the 3D effect to work, the cyan and red images need to be identical and at the same height on the screen. How far apart they are horizontally affects how far away the eye thinks the object is.

If the cyan image is to the left of the red, the object looks like it's behind the screen. If the cyan image is to the right of the red, the object looks like it's in front. How far apart the red and cyan images are controls how far behind or in front of the screen the object seems to be. In this game, we make the distance appear more extreme by making sprites smaller in the distance too.

Below you can see an example. The cat on the left is behind the screen. The middle cat, where the red and cyan images are in the same place, looks the same distance away as the bat. The cat on the right pops out. To see this in 3D, visit **www.ineasysteps.com** or the author's website – **www.sean.co.uk**

Colors that are neither red nor cyan will be distorted by the lens. Black works fine, but some colors can be uncomfortable to view so take special care when adding colored sprites to your 3D projects.

It's difficult to exactly match the color of the lens on screen, so there is sometimes a faint shadow where some of the wrong color leaks through the lens.

If your head is tilted or you look at the screen at an angle, the effect won't work. Keep your head level and sit directly in line with the screen.

Testing the anaglyph effect

Let's make a simple 3D demo. Start a new Scratch project, right-click or Shift + click the cat sprite in the Sprite List and delete it.

1 Click the **Paintbrush** button above the Sprite List to paint a new sprite. Draw any shape using only the bright red ink.

2 Right-click or Shift + click your sprite in the Sprite List and duplicate it. Click your new sprite in the Sprite List and click the **Costumes** tab. In Scratch 1.4, click the **Edit** button too. Pick the cyan ink and fill your red shape.

3 Click your **red** sprite in the Sprite List, click the Scripts tab and add this script. It puts the image in the center of the screen and sets the transparency so that the cyan and red images can overlap.

4 Click your **cyan** image in the Sprite List and add this script to it.

5 Put your glasses on and click the **green flag**. Use the left and right keys to change the distance between the images. It is easier to see the 3D effect if you do not use full screen mode for the Stage, or if you sit some distance from the screen.

Making the starry sky

Now we're ready to start making 12 Angry Aliens. We'll make a backdrop with dots at different depths. Start a new project and follow these steps:

1 Draw a red planet sprite. You could use one of the ball or planet sprites as a starting point. In Scratch 2.0, click the **convert to bitmap** button in the Paint Editor if shown. Give the sprite this short script.

2 Right-click or Shift + click your sprite and duplicate it. Edit the duplicate's costume to make it all cyan.

3 Drag both planets to the top right of the Stage, and move the cyan image so it's to the left of the red image. Make sure they're at the same height on the Stage.

4 Add the script below to the cat sprite. Click it to test it.

The pen color 100 is cyan, and the pen color 200 is red.

```
when I receive draw stars
set size to 1 %
hide
clear
set pen size to 1
point in direction 90
repeat 150
    pen up
    go to x: pick random -220 to 240 y: pick random -180 to 180
    set pen color to 200
    pen down
    move 2 steps
    pen up
    change x by pick random -20 to -30
    set pen color to 100
    pen down
    move 2 steps
    pen up
```

Use the menu in the **when I receive** block to create a message for "draw stars".

This technique enables you to use a script to draw an image precisely, but then turn that image into a sprite you can move around. The idea will be used again in the 3D Maze Explorer chapter.

Beware

Don't join this script to any other scripts.

Below: The red crosshairs image.

Drawing the crosshairs

Our game uses crosshairs to show where the player is shooting. We'll use a script to generate them. Follow these steps:

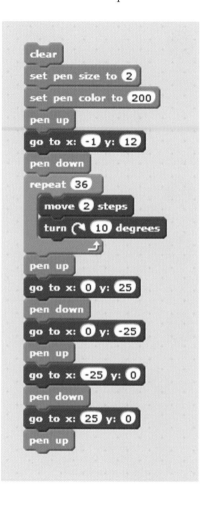

1 Add the new script on the right to the cat sprite and click it to run it.

2 Right-click or Shift + click the Stage and save its image as "red crosshairs.png" in Scratch 2.0 or "red crosshairs.gif" in Scratch 1.4.

3 Edit the script to change the number in the **set pen color to 200** block to 100 and click it again to draw the cyan crosshairs.

4 Save the Stage image as "cyan crosshairs. png" in Scratch 2.0 or "cyan crosshairs. gif" in Scratch 1.4.

5 Click the button with a folder on it above the Sprite List to add a sprite from an image on your computer. Add the red crosshairs image you just saved, and then add the cyan crosshairs as a new sprite too. In Scratch 1.4, rename the sprites to "red crosshairs" and "cyan crosshairs".

6 Click the red crosshairs in the Sprite List. Click the **Costumes** tab and in Scratch 1.4, click the **Edit** button too. Use the Eraser to delete the planets.

7 Click the Fill tool. Choose the transparent ink. In Scratch 2.0 (pictured left, below), it's in the top right of the color palette and is shown with a red diagonal line in a white box. In Scratch 1.4 (shown right, below), it's in the bottom right of the color palette and is shown with a chess board pattern.

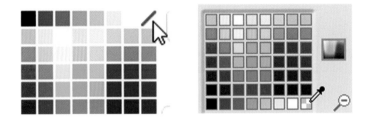

Hot tip

This script includes a section to draw a small circle by moving a few steps, turning 10 degrees, and repeating 36 times. For larger circles, you might need smaller angles of turn and more repetitions. The degree of turn multiplied by the number of repetitions should come to 360 degrees. Here's another short circle routine you can use in other projects:

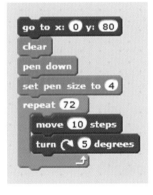

8 Click outside the crosshairs and inside the four segments in the middle to remove the white background and replace it with transparent ink, shown with a checked pattern in the Paint Editor.

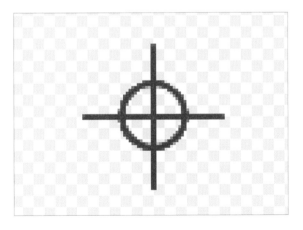

9 Edit the cyan crosshairs in the same way, so you end up with the cyan image on a transparent background too. Now we have two sprites that are identical, except for their color, and were drawn using a script.

Hot tip

As you build this script, you'll need to add new broadcast messages for "show cursor cyan", and "start aliens".

Moving the crosshairs

Now you can add the scripts to make the crosshairs move.

 Click the **Data** or **Variables** button and make these variables for all sprites: *score*, *game over*, *cursor x*, and *cursor y*. Clear the boxes beside them in the Blocks Palette.

 Add the script below to the **red** crosshairs sprite.

```
when      clicked
set  ghost ▼ effect to 50
go to x: 0 y: 0
broadcast  show cursor cyan ▼
broadcast  draw stars ▼ and wait
say  Ready... for 1 secs
say  Set... for 1 secs
say  Go! for 1 secs
set  score ▼ to 0
set  game over ▼ to 0
broadcast  start aliens ▼
repeat until  game over = 1
    broadcast  show cursor cyan ▼
    if  key left arrow ▼ pressed?  then
        change x by -10
    if  key right arrow ▼ pressed?  then
        change x by 10
    if  key up arrow ▼ pressed?  then
        change y by 10
    if  key down arrow ▼ pressed?  then
        change y by -10
```

Don't forget

The **key left arrow pressed?** block is the same as the **key space pressed?** Sensing block with a different option chosen in the menu. Remember to change all the key names and check you're using the right x and y movement blocks.

Click your **cyan** crosshairs in the Sprite List and add this script to them:

Hot tip

The red image is the one the player moves. The cyan image follows it, and is 8 steps to the right. That makes the crosshairs pop out of the screen slightly.

4 Click the **green flag** and check that you can move the crosshairs correctly after the starfield has been drawn. The game so far should look like the image below.

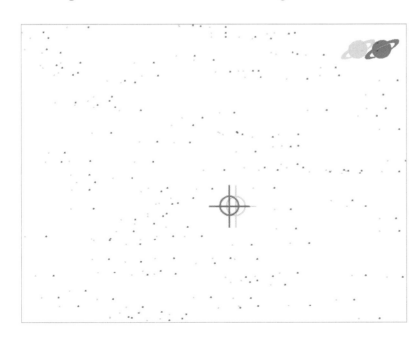

Hot tip

The **x position of red crosshairs** and **y position of red crosshairs** are Sensing blocks. You can use them to enable one sprite to check another sprite's position, direction, costume, size or volume.

To draw circles inside circles, start with the biggest first. Use the Paintbrush and paint a single dot with a large brush size. Reduce the brush size, change the color, and plot a dot inside that circle. And repeat! Below you can see my target on the Raspberry Pi.

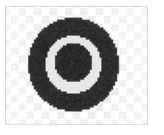

If you make the alien too big, it'll get cut off when you set the center. If that happens, click the Undo button to recover it. Click the Shrink button in the toolbar at the top of the screen and click your costume sprite in the Paint Editor to shrink it.

Adding the target sprites

Now we're ready to bring on the enemies! The process for making the sprites is similar to the one you used for the anaglyph test earlier in this chapter.

1 Click the **Paintbrush** button above the Sprite List to draw a new sprite.

2 Using only the red and white inks and the Paintbrush and Fill tools, draw an alien. If you're using a Raspberry Pi, you might need to keep your image small to avoid the game slowing down. For the Pi version, I simply made a target sign using the second largest pen size for its largest outer circle (see Hot tip).

3 Add a target sign to your sprite so players know where to shoot. The sprites will get huge as they come out of the screen and we don't want to make the game too easy!

4 Click the button to set the costume center. It's in the top right in Scratch 2.0, and it's under the color palette in Scratch 1.4. In Scratch 2.0, click the middle of your target. In Scratch 1.4, click and drag the cross to the middle of your target and then click **OK**.

5 Right-click or Shift + click your sprite in the Sprite List and duplicate it. Click your new sprite in the Sprite List and click the **Costumes** tab. In Scratch 1.4, click the **Edit** button too. Pick the cyan ink and fill your red shape.

Adding the red alien scripts

Now let's add the scripts to the aliens to get them moving.

1 Click the **Data** or **Variables** button above the Blocks Palette and make these variables for all sprites: *distance*, *alien dead*, and *alien size*. The distance variable will start at 30, which will be furthest away from the player. It's used to work out the size of the alien (in the variable *alien size*), and the separation between the red and cyan sprites.

2 Add the scripts below to the **red** alien sprite. Take care to make sure the right blocks go inside the right yellow brackets. In the **repeat until** block, add the **or** block, then two = blocks, then the two variable blocks. As you make this script, you'll need to make new broadcasts for "position blue", "hide blue" and "alien shot".

Don't forget

If you struggle to make any of the graphics needed for projects in this book, you can download them instead from **www.ineasysteps. com** or www.sean.co.uk

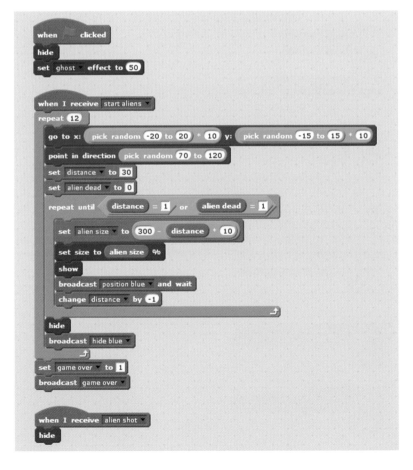

Adding the cyan alien scripts

Now let's add the scripts for the cyan target.

The red alien is the one that does most of the work in this game. The cyan one just positions itself, and hides and shows itself at the right times.

 1 Rename your red sprite to "alien red". You saw how to rename a sprite in the Gribbet! project.

2 Click the **Data** or **Variables** button above the Blocks Palette and make variables called *blue x* and *blue y* for all sprites.

3 Click the **cyan** alien sprite in the Sprite List and add the scripts below to your cyan sprite.

```
when [] clicked
hide
set ghost ▾ effect to 50


when I receive position blue ▾
set blue x ▾ to ( x position ▾ of alien red ▾ ) + 10 - distance
set blue y ▾ to ( y position ▾ of alien red ▾ )
go to x: blue x y: blue y
point in direction ( direction ▾ of alien red ▾ )
set size to alien size %
show


when I receive hide blue ▾
hide


when I receive alien shot ▾
hide
```

```
x position ▾ of alien red ▾
  x position
  y position
  direction
  costume #
  costume name
  size
  volume
```

Adding the fire button

Now we have aliens coming at us, let's get ready to shoot them!

1 Click your red crosshairs sprite in the Sprite List.

2 Click the **Sounds** tab and add two new electronic sounds: screech and zoop. In Scratch 2.0, you add a new sound by clicking the small speaker icon where it says "New sound". In Scratch 1.4, click the **Import** button.

New sound:

3 Click the **Data** or **Variables** button and make a variable for all sprites called *how far away alien is*. This stores how far away the center of the alien sprite is from the crosshairs sprite. It's a measure of how close the shot was, and is different to the alien's distance away from the player in terms of depth.

4 Clear the boxes beside all the variables in the Blocks Palette to clear them from the Stage.

5 Add the scripts below to the **red** crosshairs sprite. Click the **green flag** and have some fun blasting the aliens!

Make sure you add the right scripts to the right sprites.

```
when space ▼ key pressed
set how far away alien is ▼ to distance to alien red ▼
change score ▼ by -5
play sound zoop ▼
if    how far away alien is < 20 - distance / 2  and  alien dead = 0   then
    set alien dead ▼ to 1
    broadcast alien shot ▼
    play sound screech ▼
    change score ▼ by distance * 10


when I receive game over ▼
glide 1 secs to x: 0 y: 0
say score for 2 secs
```

Using the **say** block adds another layer of depth, because the crosshairs appear to be in front of the speech bubble.

Above: Another angry alien image I drew for the game.

Customizing the game

There are lots of ways you can adapt this simple game. Here are some suggestions for things to try.

1 If the game is too fast, add a **wait** block inside the red alien's **repeat until** block. Try a small value like 0.1 or 0.2 seconds first.

2 Add background music to up the tension! Try adding the drum machine loop and this code on the red crosshairs:

3 Make the aliens dive towards the player in pairs or larger groups. You'll need to create additional alien sprites for this, but make sure the game's still fair.

4 Add an accumulator scoring system where the player gets more points, the longer the run of uninterrupted hits is. The first alien might be worth single points, the next one double, the next one triple and so on, until the player misses one.

5 Add a spaceship that zooms across the sky in the distance, and which the player can shoot for bonus points. This might work best if the spaceship is always at the same distance away from the player.

6 Create different costumes for the alien so it looks like different aliens attack. Get the red alien to pick a random costume at the start of each round (do this near the red alien's **point in direction** block). The cyan alien can match the red alien's costume using the **costume # of alien red** block.

5 3D Artist

Introducing 3D Artist

This Scratch 2.0 project enables you to create 3D art by positioning shapes on the screen and changing their size, rotation and 3D depth. The random option generates artworks for you.

Instructions

The art package is controlled using these keys:

- **Arrow Keys.** Move the shape around the screen.

- **A and Z.** Change the 3D depth (further away and nearer).

- **O and P.** Rotate left and right.

- **S and X.** Increase and decrease the size.

- **N.** To cycle through the shapes.

- **Space.** Stamps the shape.

- **R.** Generates a random artwork for you, while you watch.

You can customize this project with your own shapes and background choice. I'm using the rays background, which makes it look like the pieces are exploding out from the middle. My image here is abstract but you can use this program to draw simple pictures (such as faces, cars, and boats) built from shapes.

This program only works in Scratch 2.0 so it won't work on the Raspberry Pi or other computers using Scratch 1.4. When you stamp a sprite in Scratch 1.4, it ignores its graphic effects. As a result, you lose the transparency that makes the 3D effect work in this project.

You'll need your 3D glasses again for this project. Remember the 3D effect only works on the computer screen. You can see a preview of this project at www. ineasysteps.com and the author's website – www.sean.co.uk

Remember to take a break when using the glasses so your eyes don't get tired.

Building 3D Artist

1 Click the **Data** or **Variables** button and make a variable called *offset* for all sprites.

2 Paint a new sprite. Draw a simple shape in red ink using the Paintbrush and Fill tools. When you've finished, click the **Costumes** tab and click the **Paint** button to paint a new costume. Repeat until you have one sprite with about six different costumes. Rename the sprite to "red".

3 Right-click or Shift + click your sprite in the Sprite List and duplicate it. Click your new sprite in the Sprite List and click the **Costumes** tab. In Scratch 1.4, click the **Edit** button too. Pick the cyan ink and fill your red shape. Repeat to color all the costumes on this sprite cyan.

4 Add the movement scripts below to your **red** sprite.

```
when up arrow key pressed          when right arrow key pressed
change y by 2                      change x by 2

when down arrow key pressed        when [flag] clicked
change y by -2                     clear
                                   set ghost effect to 50
                                   show
when left arrow key pressed        set offset to 1
change x by -2
```

5 Add the scripts below to the **red** sprite too. Make a broadcast for "stamp" when you need it.

```
when space key pressed             when I receive stamp
broadcast stamp                    stamp
```

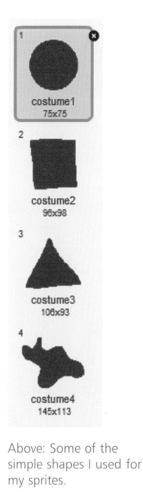

Above: Some of the simple shapes I used for my sprites.

Hot tip

The **stamp** block is used to leave a picture of the sprite on the Stage. It's like an image drawn with the pen, and can be removed using the **clear** block, which deletes all pen drawings.

...cont'd

6 Add the following scripts, also to your **red** sprite. They enable you to adjust the sprite's rotation, depth and size.

7 Add the script below to your **cyan** sprite. Make broadcasts for "cyan show", and "cyan hide" when you need them. The cyan sprite's **forever** script makes the sprite follow the red sprite and copy its size, direction and costume number continuously. It has the effect of making the cyan sprite do the same as the red sprite without needing to use broadcasts to tell it to do so.

Adding the random artist

1 Click the **Data** or **Variables** button and make new variables called *new x* and *new y*, for all sprites.

2 Add the script below to your **red** sprite.

3 Finally, let's tidy the Stage. Clear the boxes beside all the variables in the Blocks Palette and delete the cat sprite.

Hot tip

If you don't have any 3D glasses to hand, this program also works in 2D. Just leave out or delete the cyan sprite. You can have multicolored costumes on the red sprite if you're viewing in 2D, too.

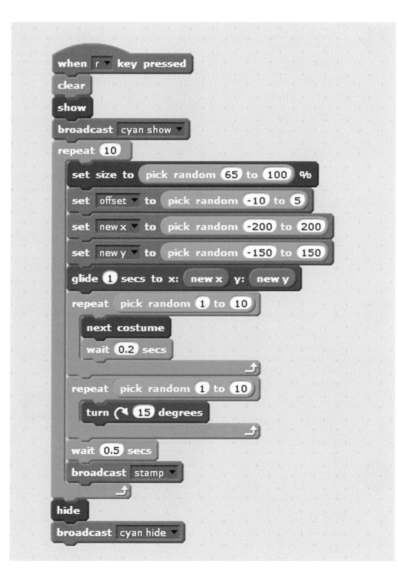

Hot tip

You could make the new artwork appear almost instantly, but it's more interesting to see how the picture is gradually built up, and how the sprite changes to make it possible.

Beware

If you generate a random artwork, it will clear the Stage before it begins.

Customizing 3D Artist

There are lots of things you can do to use 3D Artist creatively.

Hot tip

You can copy a costume from one sprite to another. Click the costume in the Costumes Area and drag it onto another sprite in the Sprite List. This is useful if you add costumes to your red sprite, because it helps you keep your cyan sprite in sync.

1 Use the simple shapes to draw a 3D picture. A car, for example, can be made of circles, rectangles and triangles. If you work out the shapes you need, you can add them to the sprite's costumes first. Make sure your cyan and red sprites are exact copies except for the color differences.

2 Try other backgrounds. The "hearts1" and "light" backgrounds work well, or you could design your own.

3 Create a more regular pattern. For example, you could stamp the sprites in a circle or use another arrangement. Here's a script that draws a spiral that you can experiment with. You'll need to make a new variable for all sprites for *degrees*.

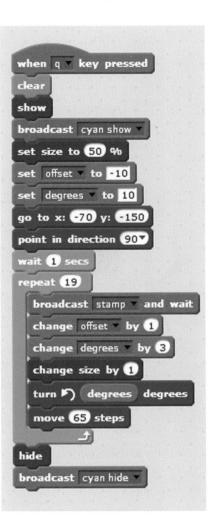

4 Remix the random art generator. Make it stamp a random number of pictures. Perhaps write the code to make sure they don't, or do, always overlap.

5 Have fun with the costume images. As long as they're one color, they can be any shape.

Above: A spiral of crazy faces created with the script on this page.

6 Space Mine 3D

In this action game, you're tasked with catching debris as it flies out of a 3D tunnel towards you. This game uses the 3D anaglyph effect to create a real sense of depth on your screen.

Beware

This project runs too slowly for the 3D effect to work on the Raspberry Pi Model B+, so use a newer Raspberry Pi or Scratch 2.0 if you can.

Introducing Space Mine 3D

Get your goggles on, and prepare for the mission of a lifetime. In Space Mine 3D, you have to pilot a spaceship to intercept debris as it flies out of a space vortex. If it spirals off into space, your space station might be hit.

You use the left and right arrow keys to move clockwise and counterclockwise around the edge of the vortex. It's a game of quick thinking: if you go the wrong way around the circle, you're more likely to miss the debris. You have 30 seconds to catch as much as you can.

The game is based around a tunnel of circles that appears to sink into the screen. The game begins with a countdown effect, where the numbers from 5 to 1 disappear into the tunnel. This adds a great sense of 3D depth before the game begins, and then the blobs of debris start flying out of the tunnel towards you.

This game uses the anaglyph 3D effect you've already explored in previous chapters, so you'll need your 3D glasses again. As before, the 3D effect doesn't work on the page but I've included some images to help you check your project is working okay.

As always, take regular breaks away from the screen and the 3D glasses to avoid getting tired eyes.

Don't forget

The 3D effect only works on the computer screen. For a sneak preview of this game in 3D, visit **www.ineasysteps.com** or the author's website.

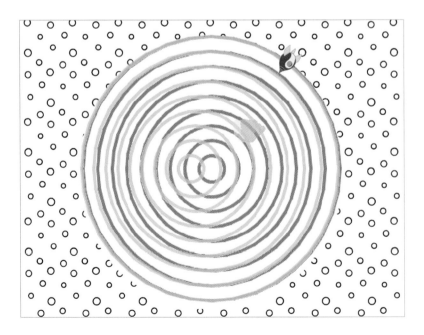

Drawing the tunnel

We'll use two separate sprites for the red circles and the cyan circles in the tunnel. This is so that we can overlap them with transparency to enable the 3D effect.

Don't forget

To make a variable, click the Data or Variables button above the Blocks Palette.

1 Make these variables for all sprites: *radius, offset, offset increase, degrees, tunnel x, tunnel y.* Clear the boxes beside them in the Blocks Palette.

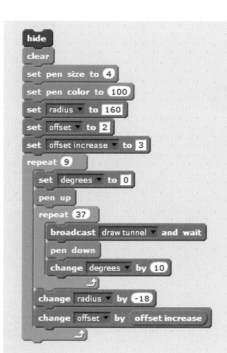

```
hide
clear
set pen size to 4
set pen color to 100
set radius ▼ to 160
set offset ▼ to 2
set offset increase ▼ to 3
repeat 9
    set degrees ▼ to 0
    pen up
    repeat 37
        broadcast draw tunnel ▼ and wait
        pen down
        change degrees ▼ by 10
    change radius ▼ by -18
    change offset ▼ by offset increase
```

2 Add the scripts on this page to the cat sprite.

3 Click the script on the right. When it finishes, right-click or Shift + click the Stage and save the image.

4 Edit the script to change the pen number from 100 to 200, and change the **set offset** and **set offset increase** blocks to both be 0. Click the script again and save the resulting image.

Hot tip

The **sin** and **cos** blocks are the same as the **sqrt** block with a different option chosen.

Below: Your two tunnel images. The cyan circles should drift off-center.

```
when I receive tunnel draw ▼
set tunnel x ▼ to ( radius * sin ▼ of degrees ) - offset
set tunnel y ▼ to ( radius * cos ▼ of degrees )
go to x: tunnel x y: tunnel y
```

Hot tip

To see how this script works, add a **wait 1 secs** and a **show** block inside the **repeat 4** bracket as the first blocks. You can add wait blocks anywhere to pause the script so you can see even more clearly what it's doing.

Drawing the numbers

One cool effect in this game is the countdown at the start, which uses large numbers that drift off down the tunnel.

1 Give the cat this new script. Don't join it to any other script.

2 Click the script and you will see a large digital number 8 drawn on the screen. If your image looks wrong, check the numbers in the **repeat** blocks and the numbers in the **turn** and **move** blocks. Make sure the **change y by -116** block is between the right yellow brackets.

3 Right-click or Shift + click the Stage and save the image.

4 Now you've drawn the images you need for this project, you can save your project and start a new one for the game.

Below: The image drawn by the script.

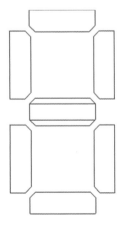

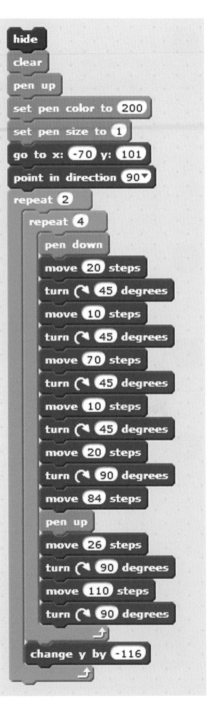

Setting up the game

Now we can start building the game as a **new project**.

1 In Scratch 2.0, add the Scratch background called "circles". In Scratch 1.4, you'll need to draw a background showing black dots or circles on white.

2 Create the following variables for all sprites: *score, target loop, target size, ship degree, countdown, count reversed*. Clear the boxes beside them in the Blocks Palette so none of them are shown on the Stage.

3 Add the script below to the cat. This is the main script that coordinates everything. It starts by drawing a big white circle in the middle of the Stage, to make a hole in the background where we will position the tunnel.

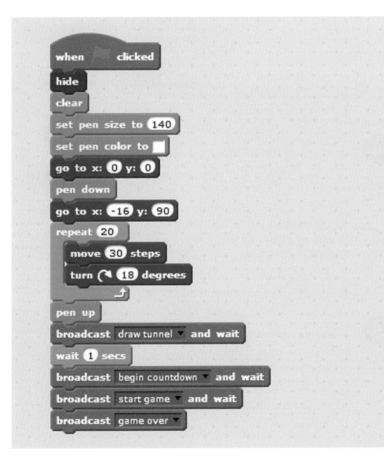

Don't forget

The maximum size of the pen is 256 in Scratch 2.0, so I've had to draw a circle with a big pen to make a bigger circle than that.

79

Don't forget

You need to make a broadcast message before you can use it. You'll need to make new broadcasts as you build this script.

Below: The script makes a white circle in the middle of the Stage.

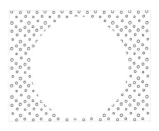

Adding the tunnel

Now we'll add the tunnel and some other game elements.

 Click the button with a folder on it above the Sprite List to add a sprite from an image on your computer. Add the red tunnel image you made, and then repeat this step to add the cyan tunnel as a separate sprite.

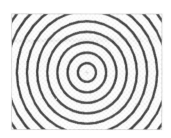 You need to fill all the white areas in the tunnel images with transparent ink. For a refresher on how to do this, start at Step 6 for drawing the crosshairs in the 12 Angry Aliens project (page 60).

 Add the script shown here to the red tunnel, and then click it and drag it onto the cyan tunnel in the Sprite List to copy it there.

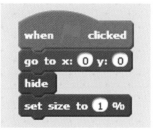

 Add any sprite to your project. It won't be shown on screen. It will be put at the middle of the tunnel so the spaceship can point towards it and so face into the tunnel. Rename the sprite to "tunnel middle" and add the script on the right to your new sprite.

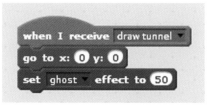

5 Click the **green flag** to test your game so far. You should see the tunnel positioned in the middle of the screen, in a clear space in the background.

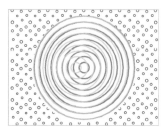

Adding the numbers

1 Click the button with a folder on it above the Sprite List to add a sprite from an image. Add your number outline.

2 Click the **Costumes** tab. In Scratch 1.4, click the **Edit** button. Choose the Fill tool and use the red ink inside all the shapes to make a filled 8 shape.

3 Choose the transparent ink and click outside the 8 to remove the white color. Click **OK** in Scratch 1.4.

4 Duplicate the costume until you have six "8" costumes. In Scratch 2.0, right-click or Shift + click the costume and choose **duplicate**. In Scratch 1.4, click the **Copy** button beside the costume in the Costumes Area.

5 Edit the first costume and erase the panes you don't need for a number 1. Repeat with the other costumes, so you have costumes for the numbers 1 to 5, plus an 8.

6 Now you need to duplicate the sprite with all its costumes. Right-click or Shift + click the sprite in the Sprite List and choose **duplicate**.

7 In the duplicated sprite, edit each costume in turn and fill all the number panes with cyan ink.

8 You should now have a red sprite and a cyan sprite. Each sprite should have the numbers 1 to 5 on it in order, plus a number 8 costume.

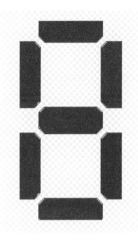

Above: The filled-in number 8 with the white surrounding color removed.

Hot tip

The extra "8" will help you with the Digital Scoreboard project later.

Hot tip

Use the same red and cyan colors as you used for 12 Angry Aliens. See the section "Testing the anaglyph effect", on page 58.

...cont'd

Hot tip

When you edit the script for the red numbers, you'll need to replace the **go to x: y:** block with a **go to mouse-pointer** block (or **go to [menu]** block in Scratch 1.4) and change the option in its menu.

Don't forget

For a reminder of how to rename a sprite, see "Drawing the frog's face" in Gribbet! on page 28.

Hot tip

The countdown won't work until you add the countdown script. If you can't wait to see it, skip to the last page of this chapter to add it now!

 Add the scripts below to the **cyan** number sprite.

 Rename the cyan number sprite to "cyan numbers".

Drag each of the scripts on the cyan number to the red number sprite in the Sprite List to copy them there.

Click the **red** number sprite in the Sprite List. Change the last few blocks under the **switch costume** block as shown below. Change the broadcast in the **when I receive block** at the top from "show countdown" to "red number".

Building the game

Now you're ready to add the player's sprite and the obstacles.

1 Add the Spaceship sprite in Scratch 2.0. In Scratch 1.4, draw a new spaceship sprite, in the "pointing up" position (see example, bottom right), and rename it to "Spaceship".

2 Add the script below to the sprite.

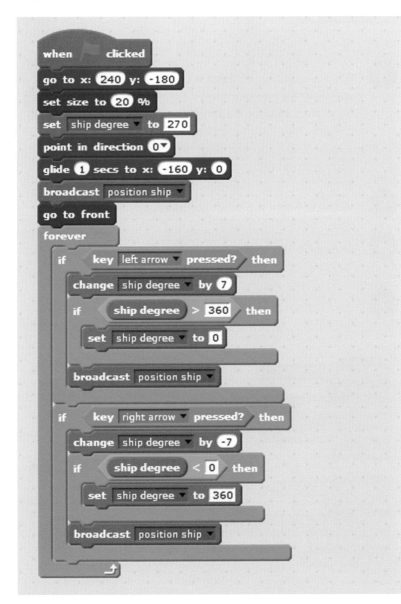

Hot tip

Sin and Cos (short for Sine and Cosine) are mathematical functions. You can use them to find the position of a point on a circle. The x position is the radius multiplied by the Sine of the number of degrees around the circle. The y position uses the Cosine instead. To put your circle somewhere other than the middle, add the coordinates for the circle middle to the calculated x and y positions.

Below: The Spaceship sprite in Scratch 2.0

...cont'd

Hot tip

When you've finished drawing your blob, use the **Set Costume Center** button in the Paint Editor to make sure the middle of the costume is the middle of your blob. See "Animating the eyes" in Gribbet! for instructions on page 31.

Hot tip

You could customize this game with different pieces of debris that move at different speeds. Make sure you keep your red and cyan sprites in sync with each other.

Don't forget

The button to paint a new sprite is the paintbrush icon above the Sprite List.

 Add the script below to the Spaceship too.

 Click the button to **paint a new sprite**. Set the brush size to maximum and draw a single spot. Use this as a guide and then draw a cyan blob about the same size beside it for the space debris. Erase the guide spot when you've finished.

 Rename your cyan sprite to "blob".

 Duplicate the sprite and edit the costume in the new sprite to make it red.

Add the scripts below to your red blob sprite.

...cont'd

8 Drag the "when I receive game over" script you just made onto the cyan blob sprite in the Sprite List.

9 Add both scripts on this page to your cyan blob sprite.

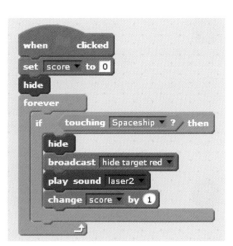

Don't forget

You need to add a sound to a sprite before you can play it. Click the Sounds tab to add the "laser2" sound to the cyan blob. Or pick another short sound if you prefer.

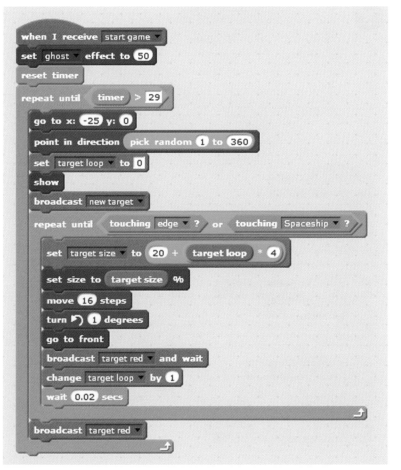

Beware

At the time of writing, the "laser2" sound doesn't work on the Raspberry Pi. Use "zoop" instead.

Hot tip

To adjust the difficulty, you can change the number in the **wait 0.02 secs** block. Bigger numbers are slower. You can also change the amount the ship degree changes by in the spaceship script to make it go faster or slower.

Adding the finishing touches

We have just a few final touches to add to complete the game.

1 Add this script to the cat. This script carries out the countdown when the game begins.

2 Add a robot sprite to your project.

3 Add the scripts below to your robot. They make it appear at the end of the game to announce the score. It's not in 3D, but it looks good floating in front of the tunnel.

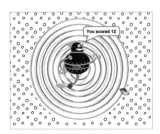

7 Maze Maker and Circuit Breaker

Introducing Maze Maker

In this project, you'll build a game called Circuit Breaker, based on randomly generated mazes. Can you chase down bugs lurking in a computer's circuit board? You can use the Maze Maker for all sorts of maze games. There are three main stages to this project:

1 You draw a grid on the Stage, and save the Stage as an image. You re-load that image as a background. It means the program can use the grid when drawing the maze, but get rid of it when it's finished without erasing the maze.

2 You generate the mazes. I'll explain this in more detail later, but you basically send a sprite to each square on the grid, taking a random route, and knock down the walls in the grid as you go. When you've finished, you remove the grid and you're left with your network of paths.

3 You add your gameplay. There are a couple of different ways to do this. For the best experience for players, I recommend you generate a stack of mazes and save them as backgrounds to use in your game, so you can switch instantly between them. Generating the mazes can take some time, although it is fun to watch!

Making the grid

Let's start by creating the background grid. Start a new project and follow these steps:

 1 Click the Stage beside the Sprite List and then click the **Backdrops** or **Backgrounds** tab. In Scratch 1.4, click the **Edit** button. Pick a color. I've gone for a nice metallic yellow. Click the Fill tool and then click the backdrop to fill the Stage with a solid color. In Scratch 1.4, click the **OK** button.

2 Click the button above the Sprite List to choose a sprite from the library. I chose the pencil in Scratch 2.0, so I can easily remember it's drawing the grid. In Scratch 1.4, there is a pencil too but it has a script already. If you use that sprite, click its script and drag it into the Blocks Palette to delete it.

3 Add the script shown on this page to your sprite. Click the script to start it and you'll see a grid appear on the screen.

4 Click the cat in the Sprite List. Click the **hide** block in the Looks part of the Blocks Palette to hide the cat.

5 Right-click or Shift + click the Stage and save a picture of the Stage. Call it "grid.png" on Scratch 2.0 or "grid.gif" in Scratch 1.4.

On the Raspberry Pi, the grid might look a bit wonky, but it will still work fine.

```
set pen size to 1
set pen color to
clear
pen up
go to x: -220 y: 160
point in direction 90
pen down
repeat 16
    move 440 steps
    move -440 steps
    change y by -20
point in direction 0
repeat 22
    move 320 steps
    move -320 steps
    change x by 20
move 320 steps
pen up
hide
```

The pencil sprite I used to draw my grid. You can use any sprite for this.

Preparing the background

To rename a backdrop in Scratch 2.0, go into the Backdrops tab and edit the name in the white box above the painting tools. To rename a backdrop in Scratch 1.4, go to the Backgrounds tab and edit the name in the dark gray box beside the small picture of the background.

Don't forget

"Backdrop" and "background" are both terms for the image behind all the sprites.

Below: This is what your grid should look like.

Now you have an image of a grid, you're ready to set up your background image and scripts.

 Click the Stage beside the Sprite List and then click the **Backdrops** or **Backgrounds** tab. Where it says New backdrop or background, click the folder icon or **Import** button and add your grid image.

 You should now have two backdrops: one that is a blank but full of color; and another that shows that same color with a grid on it. Rename the plain one to "blank". The other one should already be called "grid".

 Click the **Scripts** tab. Add these two short scripts to the Stage. Drag in the **when I receive** blocks, click the menu in them and choose **new message** to set up the new broadcasts you need.

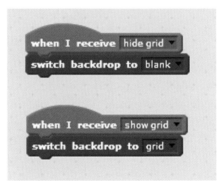

 You probably still have the grid drawn on the Stage with the pen. To remove it, click the **Pen** button in the Blocks Palette and then click the **clear** block.

5 Click the scripts on the Stage to test they are working. You should see the grid instantly appear and disappear as you click the scripts.

How the Maze Maker works

An algorithm is a set of rules to follow to solve a problem. Our algorithm to make a maze works like this:

1 It starts with a grid. Think of it as being like a set of rooms, all of them sealed up with no doors. Our maze making algorithm will ensure that every room in the maze can be visited. At least one wall on each room will get knocked down, creating a path for the player to get into that room.

2 We send our maze building sprite to a random room in the grid.

3 The sprite looks at the rooms to the left, right, up and down of it. It keeps a record of all of those that still have four walls, because those rooms haven't been visited yet. Two additional sprites are used to help with this. One of them goes to the rooms we want to check, and the other one goes to the walls of the rooms to see if they're still there or not.

4 If our maze builder sprite has rooms next to it that haven't been visited yet, it picks one at random, and moves to that room. On the way, it draws a line with the pen that overwrites the grid background, effectively demolishing a wall. We're using a nice chunky pen, so the line will be big enough for the player sprite to walk through in our finished game. It doesn't matter that bits of the grid are left showing, because we can hide the grid later by changing the backdrop, leaving just our pen-drawn paths visible.

5 If our maze builder sprite doesn't have any rooms next to it that haven't been visited, it traces its path back one step, and checks again.

6 The program repeats steps 3, 4 and 5 until it's visited every room in the grid. The grid is 22 rooms wide and 16 rooms high, so that's 352 rooms in total.

Hot tip

You can try this using correction fluid and graph paper. Follow these instructions closely, whiting out lines on the graph paper where the sprite would overwrite the grid. Alternatively, draw a grid in pencil and use an eraser to knock down the walls. It's a great way to understand how the program works.

Hot tip

The algorithm doesn't need to do anything special at the edge of the grid. That's because when it tests a space outside the grid, it only has one wall (the edge of the grid). It's treated like a room that's been visited because it has fewer than four walls. The algorithm either goes somewhere else or backtracks, so it continues building the maze within the grid.

The Button1 sprite in Scratch 2.0.

To rename a sprite in Scratch 2.0, click it in the Sprite List, and click the **i** button on it. Click and edit its name in the white box at the top of the information pane that opens. In Scratch 1.4, click and edit the name in the dark gray box above the Scripts Area.

Below: The cat should sit neatly inside the grid, not touching any of the lines.

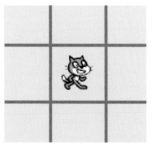

Checking rooms and walls

This is quite a complex program and it would be frustrating to get to the end, find it doesn't work properly and not know where to start looking for errors. We'll build this program up gradually, then, and test it as we go. This process will give you an idea of how I wrote it too: trying small sections, checking they worked, and then adding new bits.

1 You should have a cat sprite, called Sprite1, in your project without any scripts on it. The cat is going to be our maze builder sprite. Click it in the Sprite List and give it the script below. Assembling the **go to x: y:** block might be tricky: start with the **go to x: y:** block, then add a + block in each hole, then the * blocks in the left hole of the + blocks, and finally the **pick random** blocks.

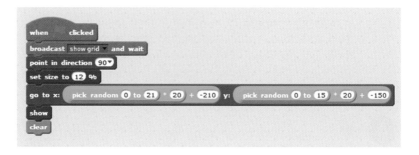

2 Click the green flag button above the Stage. You should see the grid with the cat positioned in a random room in it. If there's no grid, check your broadcast names and the scripts that you put on the Stage earlier. If the cat appears in strange places, check all the numbers in the **go to x: y:** block. Click the green flag a few times until you're happy the cat positioning works.

3 Add the sprite Button1 if you're using Scratch 2.0 or baseball1 in Scratch 1.4. Rename the sprite to 'move checker'. Give the sprite the script shown on the right.

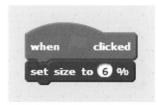

4 Add the script below to the move checker sprite too. Use the **broadcast and wait** block, and not the ordinary **broadcast** block. It stops the script from moving forwards until the code the broadcast triggers has finished.

In Step 4 you add some broadcasts. No scripts are listening for those broadcasts, so they won't do anything, yet. But their moment will come, very soon!

```
when I receive check move options ▾
go to Sprite1 ▾
change x by 20
broadcast test walls ▾ and wait
go to Sprite1 ▾
change x by -20
broadcast test walls ▾ and wait
go to Sprite1 ▾
change y by -20
broadcast test walls ▾ and wait
go to Sprite1 ▾
change y by 20
broadcast test walls ▾ and wait
```

5 Click the **green flag** to position your cat sprite and set the size of your move checker sprite.

6 Click the script you just added to the move checker sprite. You should see the tiny sprite visit the four rooms that share a wall with the cat sprite's room (at the top, bottom, left, and right of that room). If not, use a **wait 1 secs** block to slow it down, as explained in the Hot tip.

If your test in Step 6 is too fast to see, you can add this script to your checker sprite to slow it down. Remember to delete this script when you've finished, though!

```
when I receive test walls ▾
wait 1 secs
```

93

...cont'd

The Flower Shape sprite in Scratch 2.0. In Scratch 1.4, you'll use the tennisball to check walls.

Hot tip

For the color box in the **touching color** blocks, click on the color box in the block and then click your grid on the Stage. You need to match your grid color exactly.

Hot tip

The **x position of move checker** block is among the Sensing blocks. You'll need to change the sprite name in it. The y position block is the same block, but with the first menu item also changed.

7 We need a sprite to test the walls of our rooms too. Let's set that up now, using the following steps. Add the Flower Shape sprite in Scratch 2.0 or tennisball in Scratch 1.4. Give it the script to the right.

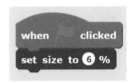

8 Make a variable called *walls* for all sprites. Make two lists called *x options* and *y options*. Select the options to make these lists for all sprites.

9 Add the script below to the Flower or tennisball:

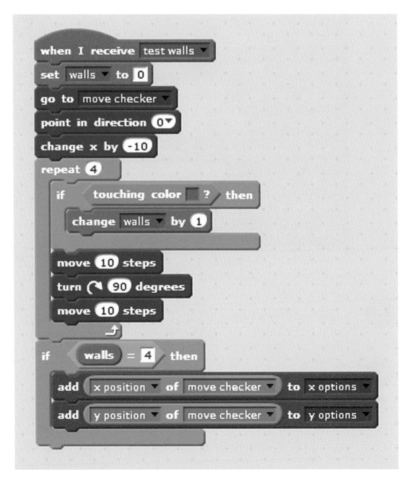

Understanding how it works

Three sprites work together to build our maze. Here's a quick explanation of how they cooperate to get the job done.

The cat sprite visits each square on the grid, building the path of our maze. It has to work out which rooms next to it haven't been visited yet. To do that, it calls on the help of the move checker sprite, which is green in our picture above. It will do this with the broadcast "check wall options", but we haven't added that code yet.

The move checker sprite goes to where the cat is, and then jumps into a room next to the cat. When it gets there, it calls on the help of the test walls sprite, shown in purple above (the Flower Shape sprite). It does this with the broadcast "test walls".

The test walls sprite goes to where move checker is, but then goes to the left, right, top and bottom edge of the room to see if there are walls there (using the **touching color** block). It uses the variable *walls* to keep count of how many walls it finds for the room. If there are four walls, the room is unvisited, so it adds the position of the middle of the room (the x and y coordinates) to the lists *x options* and *y options*. The middle of the room is where the move checker sprite is, so it uses its coordinates for this.

The move checker sprite visits all four rooms connected to the cat's room and gets the test walls sprite to check the walls for them all. Only then can the cat decide where to move next.

Hot tip

Breaking the problem down into smaller chunks can often make it easier to solve. In this case, we've used different sprites for visiting rooms, checking rooms and checking walls. Imagine how complicated your scripts might get if the cat did all the work here!

Don't forget

If you're using Scratch 1.4, your sprites will look different to the ones in the example here. The idea's the same, though.

Don't forget

Untick the boxes beside walls, x options and y options in the Blocks Palette when you've finished testing.

Hot tip

It is possible to have bugs that still result in four list items, so this test doesn't guarantee your program is working. But errors like that are rare. If you see four items, that's a good sign that it's working.

Don't forget

The Eraser tool looks like a rectangular box. When you leave the mouse pointer on one of the Art tools for a moment, a tip appears to tell you what that tool does.

Below: Erasing a line in the grid in Scratch 2.0 (grid has been magnified).

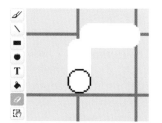

Testing the wall checker

Now let's confirm that our wall checker script is working correctly by running some simple tests.

 Click the **green flag** button. If the cat appears in one of the rooms at the edge of the grid, click again. Edge rooms only have three movement options and we should check the script can find all the movement options first.

 Click the move checker sprite in the Sprite List and click its long script once.

 In the Data or Variables section of the Blocks Palette, tick or check the boxes beside *x options* and *y options* to show them on the Stage, if you need to. There should be four items in each of these lists. That means it's working! The script has checked the rooms around the cat, and found four rooms that still have all their walls.

 Click the Stage beside the Sprite List and click the Backdrops or Backgrounds tab. In Scratch 2.0, Shift + click your grid and duplicate it. In Scratch 1.4, click the **Copy** button and the **Edit** button on your copy. Now erase a few walls in the **grid copy** you made. It doesn't matter that the eraser shows as white on your yellow background.

 Click the **delete all of y options** and **delete all of x options** blocks in the Blocks Palette to empty your lists. You'll need to change the menus in them first.

 Drag the cat on the Stage to a room with missing walls.

 Click the move checker sprite in the Sprite List and click its "check move options" script. This time, how many options are in the lists? The number of options should be the number of rooms beside the cat with all their walls. If not, check your "testing walls" script.

Repeat steps 5, 6 and 7 a few times using different rooms with different walls missing (top, bottom, left, right).

Preparing for the cat code

Before we add the main maze generator script to the cat sprite, we need to tidy a few things up, both to remove the effects of our testing and to set up the variables and lists we'll need when we add our maze making script.

1 The maze making is much, much slower if our sprites are shown on screen. On the *move checker* and *test walls* sprites (pictured, right), join a **hide** block to their **when green flag clicked** scripts, underneath the **set size** blocks. The **hide** block is in the Looks part of the Blocks Palette.

2 The cat needs to work undercover too, to speed things up. We'll add a **hide** block shortly, but your script will be tidier if you remove the **show** block that's in its script now. Remember that when you drag blocks out of a script, any blocks joined to it go too. So you'll need to drag the **show** block out, and then detach the **clear** block from underneath it. Drag the **clear** block back into your script again.

3 Our cat code needs two new variables: *rooms visited* – used to count how many rooms the cat has visited, so it knows when it's reached them all; and *path chosen* – used to decide which of the possible routes it's taking. Click the **Data** or **Variables** button, and then make both variables for all sprites.

4 The cat needs two lists too: *visited x* and *visited y* – used to remember the coordinates of the rooms the cat has visited. This enables it to trace its path back when it needs to. Make both lists for all sprites.

5 In the Blocks Palette, clear the boxes beside all the variables and lists. Otherwise, they'll be in the way on the Stage and will get in the way of the grid.

Hot tip

Here's an expert tip for deleting blocks in the middle of a script without dragging the attached blocks you want back in again: Find the block you want to delete, click the block below it, and drag and drop it above the one you're going to delete. The one you want to get rid of is now at the bottom of the script, so when you drag it out, nothing goes with it.

Beware

If your tests haven't worked, go back and fix your code before going any further!

You'll need the **repeat until**, **broadcast and wait** and **if...then...else** (also known as **if...else**) blocks for this script. Don't use the similar **repeat**, **if** or **broadcast** blocks.

Don't forget

The grid is 22 rooms wide by 16 rooms tall. That's why the cat keeps going until the *rooms visited* variable is equal to 22 times 16. I could have just put the answer in the code, but the sum provides more explanation for anyone reading the program.

Hot tip

Click the green flag and prepare to be, ahem, amazed! Be patient too. It takes a while, and sometimes it doesn't look like it's doing much.

Making the Maze Maker

Now our sprites are all ready, it's time to add our maze generator scripts to the cat sprite. Click the cat sprite in the Sprite List and then follow these steps.

 1   Add the following blocks to the end of your cat's script. They mostly set up the pen ready to draw the maze paths.

```
set pen color to 80
set pen size to 18
pen up
hide
set rooms visited to 1
```

2   Now add the following blocks to the cat's script. They do the job of moving the cat around the grid to visit each room, building the maze as it goes. The **if...then...else** block is just called **if...else** in Scratch 1.4.

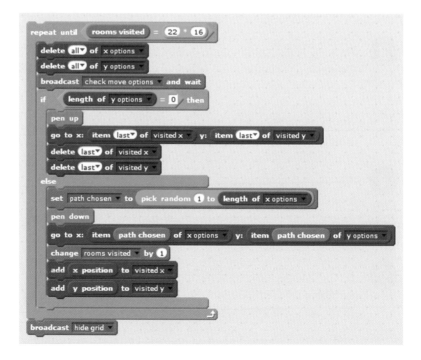

Adding components

Let's add components at the end of the maze paths to make the screen look more like a circuit board.

1 Click the cat sprite in the Sprite List, and click the **Costumes** tab. In Scratch 2.0, click the button to choose a costume from the library, and add "star2" from the Things category. In Scratch 1.4, click the **Import** button, go into the Things folder, and add the "button" sprite.

2 Create a variable called *reversing counter* for all sprites. Clear its box in the Blocks Palette to remove it from the Stage so it's not in the way.

3 Create the script below on the cat. In Scratch 1.4, use the costume name "button" in place of "star2".

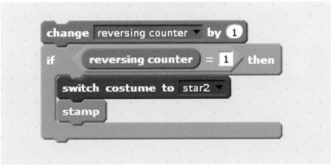

4 Take a look at your maze maker script (see Step 2 on the facing page). Find the **if...then...else** command. The new script you just made belongs in the top bracket. Drag it in, just under the **delete last of visited y** block.

5 Whenever the sprite moves forwards, you need to reset the reversing counter. Add the block below into the bottom half of the **if...then...else** bracket, under the **add y position to visited y** block.

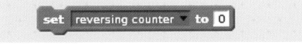

Hot tip

Click the green flag to draw a new maze with your components stamped in place.

Beware

Add this new component image as a costume on the cat sprite, not as a new sprite.

Hot tip

In Chapter Eight, you'll see how to explore your randomly generated mazes by walking through them. For best results, don't use mazes with components for that. To turn off the components, just drag out the **stamp** block here and put it back when you want them back in again.

Saving mazes

You can build a game onto the end of the maze creation script. That would make every game unique, but it takes so long to draw the maze, that you couldn't really get much action going. The mazes aren't hard enough that players would want to play one maze for very long, either. You can make a faster, multi-level game by generating the mazes, saving them as images and then using them as costumes on a sprite so you can switch between them instantly.

 Click the **green flag** to generate a maze.

 When the maze has been made, Shift + click or right-click the Stage. Choose the menu option to **Save picture of the Stage**.

3 Enter a filename, such as "maze.png" in Scratch 2.0 or "maze.gif" in Scratch 1.4. To avoid overwriting any mazes, use filenames like 'maze1', 'maze2', 'maze3' and so on.

4 And repeat! How many mazes do you need? 10 should be enough, but the game would have more replayability with extra mazes. You can always add more later.

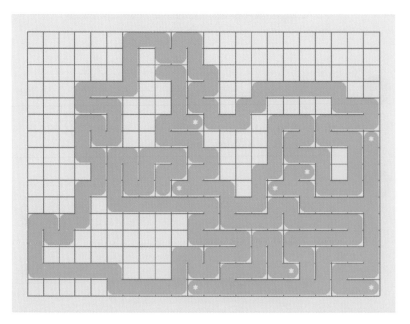

Right: A picture of the maze generation in progress. The grid is still shown. When the maze has finished drawing, the grid is taken away.

Displaying mazes

Now you have a program that makes mazes, and a set of mazes saved as image files. It's time to build the Circuit Breaker game, starting with the sprite that displays the maze.

 1 Save Maze Maker and start a new Scratch project for the game. Edit the background and fill it with yellow.

 2 Click the button to paint a new sprite. It's above the Sprite List.

 3 In **Scratch 2.0**, click the button to upload a costume. It looks like a folder with an arrow and is to the left of the editing window. Bring in your first maze image. Then repeat until you've added them all. When you've finished, delete the empty first costume.

 4 In **Scratch 1.4**, click the **Import** button. It is towards the top left of the Paint Editor. Choose your first maze image, and click the **OK** button to add it, and **OK** again to exit the editor. Click the **Costumes** tab. Click the **Import** button at the top to bring in your next maze, and repeat that step until you've added them all.

 5 Click the **Scripts** tab and add the following scripts to your sprite. Change the 10 in the **pick random** block to the number of mazes you have.

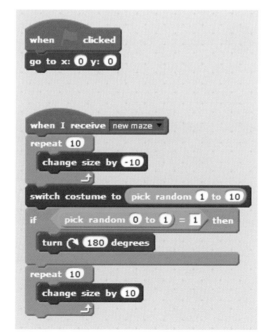

Beware

Make sure you save your maze creation program before you start to make your new program now.

Hot tip

Click each of these scripts to test them. The first one centers the maze on screen. The second one uses a nice transition effect to change to a random maze.

Hot tip

I've included some blocks to sometimes rotate the maze by 180 degrees. A maze looks quite different upside down, so this doubles the number of puzzles in your game for no extra work.

Adding the bug

This is probably the only time you'll want to add a bug to your program! This is the enemy players will hunt down in the maze.

 1 Add a new sprite to your project from the library. In Scratch 2.0, use Beetle. In Scratch 1.4, use insect1-a.

 2 Add another costume to your sprite. In Scratch 2.0, click the **Costumes** tab and then click the button to choose a costume from the library. Choose lightning. In Scratch 1.4, there isn't a suitable costume available, so click the **Costumes** tab and **Paint** a costume and rename it to "lightning".

 3 Click the Scripts tab and add a script to the sprite to hide it when the game begins:

 4 Click the **Sounds** tab and add your favorite bug squishing sound effect. I've used buzz whir. Add the following script to your bug sprite too.

```
when I receive caught bug ▼
switch costume to lightning ▼
turn ↻ 15 degrees
set size to 30 %
play sound buzz whir ▼ until done
turn ↺ 15 degrees
hide
```

5 Click the **Data** or **Variables** button above the Blocks Palette and make two variables for all sprites: *bug x* and *bug y*. We'll use them to temporarily remember the random position generated for our bug. Clear the boxes beside their names in the Blocks Palette.

6 Add the script below to your bug sprite. For the green operators in the **set bug x** and **set bug y** blocks, drag them like this: **+**, then *****, and then **pick random** on top.

If you're using Scratch 1.4, change the name of the costume in the switch costume block to insect1-a.

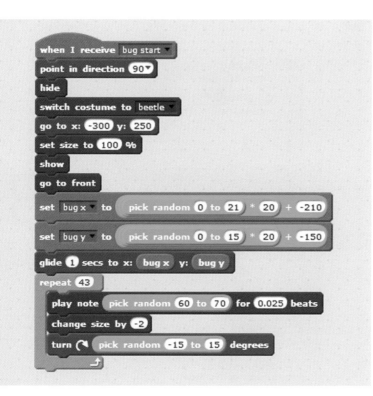

You can use a different sprite for your enemy, but make sure it fits within the maze. If not, adjust the number of repeats in the script here to change how much it shrinks by, so it fits between the lines.

7 Click this script to test it. It should make the bug crawl into a random maze position.

8 Test your *caught bug* script by clicking that. It should change the bug to its splatted costume, play a sound and hide it.

Adding the player's sprite

For our player, we'll use the cat which should already be Sprite1. Click the cat sprite in the Sprite List and follow these steps:

 1 Click the **Data** or **Variables** button. Make six variables for all sprites: *score*, *player x*, *player y*, *old x*, *old y* and *timer*. Clear the boxes beside their names in the Blocks Palette.

 2 Click the **Sounds** tab and add a 'Game Over' sound effect. I'm using space ripple in Scratch 2.0. Guitarstrum in Scratch 1.4 works well too.

 3 Add the following scripts to your sprite.

Hot tip

For the best effect, I recommend changing the Stage background to the same yellow color as the circuit board. Check back to see how you did this when making the grid if you need a reminder.

Hot tip

For the **touching color** block here, pick the color from your maze walls. It has to match exactly!

```
when I receive position cat
go to x: -240 y: 0
set size to 12 %
show
go to front
repeat until  not  touching color [ ] ?
    set player x to ( pick random 0 to 21 ) * 20 + -210
    set player y to ( pick random 0 to 15 ) * 20 + -150
    go to x: player x y: player y
```

```
when   clicked
set timer to 120
repeat until ( timer = 0 )
    change timer by -1
    wait 1 secs
broadcast hide bug
play sound space ripple
set size to 100 %
glide 1 secs to x: 0 y: 0
think join You scored score for 2 secs
stop all
```

Click the "position cat" script to test it. You should see the cat go to a random location, not touching a wall.

5 Add the main game script shown below to your cat.

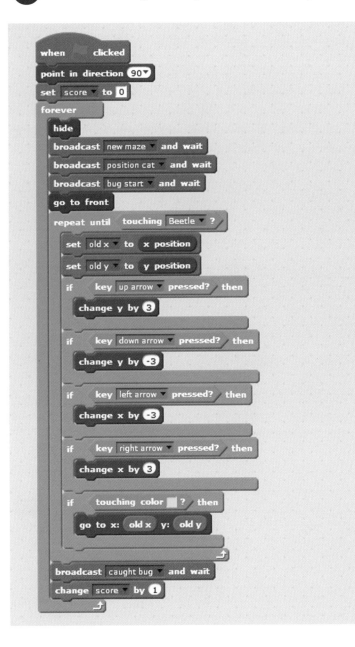

Hot tip

In Scratch 1.4, replace the **touching Beetle** block with "touching Sprite3", which should be your bug/squashed effect sprite.

Hot tip

For the **touching color** block, click the square of color in it, then click the maze wall. This bit of the script stops the player walking through walls.

...cont'd

 6 We don't often show variables on the Stage, but it will be useful for players to be able to see the time remaining and their score so far as they progress through the game. Click the **Data** or **Variables** button in the Blocks Palette. Tick or check the box beside the *score* and *timer* variables so they appear on the Stage. Double-click the variables' boxes until they just show a number. Drag the timer to the top left, and the score to the top right of the screen. Make sure they don't totally cover the maze wall at the top, otherwise the player might be able to leave the maze.

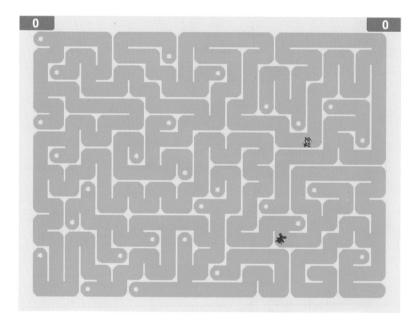

Beware

Make sure you put the variable boxes high enough up on the Stage so there is a clear line of wall color between the path and the box. Otherwise players might be able to run out of the maze into the variable box!

7 Two final blocks and you're done! Take care though: these blocks don't go on the cat sprite. They go on the **bug**.

8 It's time to play! Click the **green flag**, and see how many bugs you can squash in two minutes!

More amazing ideas to try

Congratulations on finishing this project! Here are some suggestions for ways you can customize it, improve on it, and reuse bits of it.

Hot tip

You could also print mazes out to solve on paper. Save them as images first.

- Experiment with different maze shapes. If a room in the grid doesn't have four visible walls, it doesn't get visited and doesn't get a path drawn to it. For example, here's a grid where I've shaved the corners of the grid off with the eraser. You could also add images in the middle, even using sprites to position them randomly before generation begins (they have to hide at least one wall to keep the cat out of a room). Change the number in the **repeat until** block of the cat's main maze generation script to take away any rooms that are obscured by an image, otherwise the maze generation would never end. The cat could never visit those rooms, but wouldn't stop until it had!

Don't forget

Remember you can save your mazes to use in different games. In the next chapter, you'll see how you can explore your mazes in 3D.

107

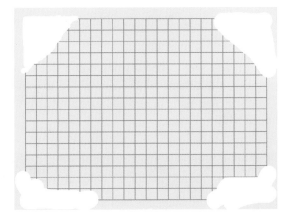

- What if touching the walls drained your energy? You'd have to go much more slowly around the maze then! Perhaps you could draw a red spot at the end of the path in place of the components. It could enable players to top up their energy when they touch it. Use the **touching color** block to check when to increase an *energy* variable.

- You could give players more points when they catch a bug more quickly. That would make the game more rewarding to play again and again, and to play with friends. Or maybe catching a bug could increase the timer?

Don't forget

You can change the difficulty of the game by giving players more or less time to catch bugs. Adjust the starting value of the timer variable in the cat's script.

...cont'd

Hot tip

In Chapter Eight we'll see another way we can use these random mazes, when we make the 3D Maze Explorer project.

- You can use the player's timer script with small adjustments in pretty much any game! Just take out the **broadcast** block.

- Customize the game with your own artwork and theme. Take care to make sure your sprites still fit inside the maze okay. You might need to adjust the numbers in the **set size** blocks.

- You could give the cat a special power to walk through walls sometimes, perhaps wiping them out with the pen.

- The **distance to** Sensing block can be used to tell how close one sprite is to another. Perhaps the cat (or the bug!) could make a sound when the cat gets closer to the bug.

- Music can heighten the tension. Why not see if you can add some music that repeats in the background while the game is played? Or maybe add a few well chosen sound effects to mark the passing of time.

- Try different numbers in the **set pen color** block on the cat sprite to paint a different colored maze. 185 gives you a pink color. I combined it with my edited grid on the previous page to make the Brain Maze.

Beware

If you use odd shaped mazes, make sure the bug is positioned inside the maze. The script that positions the cat includes a check to make sure it's not in a wall (or outside the maze). It's not needed for the basic mazes we've used so far, but it's there for odd shaped mazes and so you can reuse it to safely position the bug.

8 3D Maze Explorer

Introducing Maze Explorer

In Chapter Seven, you saw how to generate random mazes. In this chapter, you'll see how to display them from the player's point of view. With this game, you can:

- **Explore your mazes.** Whether you design mazes on paper and type in the relevant code, or use the built-in art editor in Scratch, you can make your own maze design, and enable players to solve it by walking around a 3D environment.

- **Explore random mazes.** Use some of the maze images you generated last chapter, or download some from my website if you haven't completed the previous project yet.

- **Hide rewards.** I've hidden some delicious cakes in my test maze, but you could easily hide a key to unlock the door, or anything else that takes your fancy.

The game shows up to six layers of depth, looking into the distance. Beyond that, the corridor is dark. At each layer of depth, and on each side of the maze, you can have either a passageway or a wall. That gives you plenty of directions to explore. The game relies on precise sizing and positioning of the images for the perspective to work, so we'll use the pen to draw them.

In the next chapter, you'll add the finishing touches to this game.

Beware

This game works but is noticeably slower on the Raspberry Pi 2 Model B and Raspberry Pi 3 Model B. It runs too slow on the Model B+ to be playable. If possible, use Scratch 2.0 on another computer instead. If you are using a Pi, I suggest you download the game and test it'll run okay for you before you build your version.

Hot tip

You don't need your 3D glasses for this game.

Creating the wall images

We'll begin by making the sprites we'll need in this game. Start a new Scratch project and follow these steps to make the walls:

1 Add this script to the cat. Click the script to draw the wall, like the image below.

2 Shift + click (in Scratch 2.0) or right-click (in Scratch 1.4) the Stage. Save the image as "wall.png" (in Scratch 2.0) or "wall.gif" (in Scratch 1.4).

3 Click the button above the Sprite List to upload a sprite from a file and load your wall image.

4 Click the **Costumes** tab. In Scratch 1.4, click the **Edit** button. Pick the transparent ink. Select the Fill tool and click outside the lines to make the sprite background invisible. Fill the rectangle part of the wall in brown, and the slanted area in orange.

5 Click the **Looks** button and click the **hide** block to hide the sprite. The pen drawing remains.

```
hide
clear
pen up
set pen size to 4
set pen color to 30
go to x: -108 y: 176
pen down
go to x: -108 y: -176
go to x: 28 y: -176
go to x: 28 y: 176
go to x: -108 y: 176
go to x: 28 y: 176
go to x: 108 y: 122
go to x: 108 y: -122
go to x: 28 y: -176
```

Hot tip

If you can't remember how to use transparent inks, take a look at page 18 in the Magic Mirror project.

Hot tip

Slightly different colors for the wall panels look like the effect of lighting. Radically different colors won't make sense, because the same piece of wall is shown using different panels depending on where the player is standing.

Beware

The numbers in the Motion blocks are really important in this script. The position and dimensions of the image affect how well the walls lock together.

...cont'd

Beware

This is a new script. Don't join it to your wall drawing script or any other script.

Hot tip

Notice I'm not using the green flag yet? That's to make sure we only run one drawing script at a time.

Below: The front wall sprite. It almost, but not quite, fills the Stage when viewed at full size.

We'll use a separate sprite for the blocking wall in front of the player. Again, we'll use a script to draw it.

6 Give the cat this script. Click the script to draw the wall. It looks like a big yellow empty box.

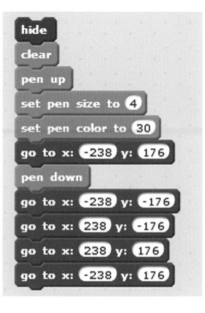

7 Shift + click (in Scratch 2.0) or right-click (in Scratch 1.4) the Stage. Save the image as "front wall. png" (in Scratch 2.0) or "front wall.gif" (in Scratch 1.4).

8 Click the folder button above the Sprite List to upload a sprite from a file and load your new front wall file.

9 Edit the costume and fill the middle of the shape with the same brown color you used for the flat surface of the side wall. This is the surface of the blocking wall. At the top and bottom of the image is a thin stripe of white. Pick the transparent ink and select the Fill tool. Click at the top and the bottom of the image. It's easier if you zoom in to see the white space, as I have below:

Creating the door

The maze will have only one exit, but it can be viewed from three positions (in front, to the left, to the right). We'll need three door images to show it throughout the game.

1. Click the **Looks** button and click the **hide** block.

2. Click the cat in the Sprite List and add the new script on the right. Click the script.

3. Save the Stage image. Use the filename "door front.png" in Scratch 2.0 or "door front.gif" in Scratch 1.4.

```
hide
clear
pen up
set pen size to 4
set pen color to 30
go to x: 30 y: -74
pen down
go to x: 30 y: 74
go to x: -30 y: 74
go to x: -30 y: -74
go to x: 30 y: -74
```

4. Click the button above the Sprite List to upload a sprite from a file and bring in your door image.

5. Click the **Costumes** tab. In Scratch 1.4, click the **Edit** button beside your costume too.

6. Select the transparent ink. Select the Fill tool on the left and click outside the lines. The outside should fill with a checked pattern, which means that area is transparent. The transparency stops the door sprite from hiding the wall behind.

7. Choose a color for the inside of your door and fill it in. I chose a deep red color that contrasts nicely with the orange and brown used for the walls.

Hot tip

If you're feeling creative, you could try drawing a half-open door in the frame, or even the view outside. But it'll get tricky when you have to do the same thing from a side view later!

113

Beware

The numbers in the script are important here for the size and positioning of the door. A small mistake here might lead to strange results when the images are combined to show the maze.

...cont'd

You need to make two images that show the door on the left and right. I'm sure you'll find this process quite familiar by now!

8 Click your door sprite in the Sprite List. Click the **Looks** button above the Blocks Palette and then click the **hide** block to hide the sprite. The pen drawing will remain.

9 Use the script on the right to draw the left door. Add it to the **cat** as a new script and click the script.

10 Save the Stage image as "door left.png" in Scratch 2.0 or "door left.gif" in Scratch 1.4.

11 Repeat this process with the second script on this page, this time saving the file as "door right.png" or "door right.gif".

12 Click your door sprite in the Sprite List, and click the **Costumes** tab.

13 Where it says New Costume, click the folder icon in Scratch 2.0 or **Import** button in Scratch 1.4 to upload a costume from a file. Add both your left and right door images.

14 Edit the door costumes in the same way you edited the front door and wall: make the area outside the door transparent, and fill the door in with color. Red worked well in my color scheme.

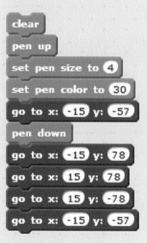

Above: This is what the left door looks like. Trust me: it'll make sense when we start putting the images together! The right door is a mirror image of this one.

Beware

Don't add the left and right doors as new sprites. You want to end up with a single door sprite, with three costumes for front, left and right.

Creating the sky and floor

You could just use a plain background, but I found the maze looks more striking with a deep blue sky and a vibrant green floor. Feel free to experiment with your own choice of sky and floor color.

Hot tip

The advantage of using a background image is that it remains after a "clear" command. If we used these drawing instructions in the game instead, we'd need to redraw every time the player moved.

1 Add the script on this page to the **cat** sprite and click it to draw the background. It should look like the picture on this page. The line across the middle is used for darkness when the passage goes beyond six layers of depth.

2 Shift + click or right-click the Stage and save the image as "sky and floor.png" in Scratch 2.0 or "sky and floor.gif" in Scratch 1.4.

3 Click the Stage icon beside the Sprite List. Click the **Backdrops** or **Backgrounds** tab.

4 In Scratch 2.0, click the New backdrop button with a folder on it to upload from a file. In Scratch 1.4, click the **Import** button. Add the image you just made to add your pen drawing as a background for the project.

```
set pen shade to 50
set pen color to 140
set pen size to 162
go to x: -240 y: 100
clear
pen down
go to x: 240 y: 100
set pen color to 65
pen up
go to x: -240 y: -100
pen down
go to x: 240 y: -100
set pen shade to 0
set pen color to 1
set pen size to 38
pen up
go to x: -240 y: 0
pen down
go to x: 240 y: 0
```

Don't forget

If you can't get one of these drawing scripts working, you can download the images and then pick up the project again.

Positioning the left walls

Each wall is a separate sprite, so you'll end up with 12 wall sprites (six on the left, six on the right). Let's position the left walls:

1 Click the **Data** or **Variables** button above the Blocks Palette. Click the button to **Make a list**. Make a list called *wall sizes*, and another list called *wall positions*. These should be for all sprites.

2 The lists have boxes that appear on the Stage to show the list contents. Click the + button in the bottom left of the *wall positions* box, and in Scratch 1.4 also click the orange text entry box. You can now type numbers into the list. Add the numbers shown below. Press Enter when you finish typing each one to move to the next one. This list is used for the x position (the position from left to right) of each chunk of wall. The list goes from nearest to furthest.

3 Do the same to add the data to the *wall sizes* list. This list is for the size of each wall. Walls are smaller further away.

4 Clear the boxes beside the list blocks in the Blocks Palette to hide them from the Stage.

Hot tip

We could have used blocks to add this data to the lists. None of these numbers will change during the game, though, so it's simpler and quicker to add them in this way.

Hot tip

Drag the list boxes on the Stage if necessary so you can see them clearly.

Beware

Pay careful attention to the numbers here. If your maze looks wrong, with walls in the wrong place, you might have made a mistake here.

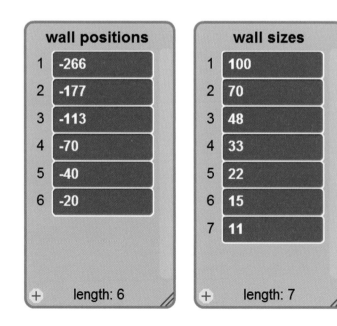

wall positions		wall sizes	
1	-266	1	100
2	-177	2	70
3	-113	3	48
4	-70	4	33
5	-40	5	22
6	-20	6	15
		7	11
+	length: 6	+	length: 7

...cont'd

5 Click the **side wall** sprite in the Sprite List.

6 Click the **Data** or **Variables** button. Click the button to make a variable and create a variable called *wall number*. Select the option to make the variable **for this sprite only**. Clear its box in the Blocks Palette.

The wall number variable must be for this sprite only. The program won't work otherwise.

New Variable

Variable name: wall number

○ For all sprites ● For this sprite only

OK   Cancel

If you make a variable for one sprite only, you can have other variables with the same name in your project. This is handy when you're duplicating sprites, because it means they can use identical code and variable names, but store different values in their variables. When you duplicate a sprite, its variables are also duplicated.

7 Add the script below to your side wall sprite. To set up the first block, add the block **when I receive message1** (or **when I receive** in Scratch 1.4)

to your sprite. Then click the menu in it, choose "new message" or "new/edit", and then type in your message of "place walls". For the **go to x: y:** block, start by adding **go to x:0 y:0**. Then add the list block **item 1 of [list name]** and drop it into the x hole. Change the list name if necessary. Finally, drop the variable block *wall number* on top of the number 1. Use a similar process with the **set size to 100%** block.

```
when I receive place walls
set wall number to 1
go to x: item wall number of wall positions y: 0
set size to item wall number of wall sizes %
```

The broadcast blocks are yellow in Scratch 1.4, and can be found in the Control section of the Blocks Palette.

117

...cont'd

Beware

The wall numbers are always 1 more than the broadcast numbers. For example, the sprite that uses wall number 3 must respond to broadcast "show left 2". This is because items in a list are numbered from 1 (not 0), and the wall number is used to find the sizes and positions in the lists. Our broadcasts respond to the distance the player can see, with zero meaning they're up against a wall.

8 There are two other scripts that our side wall sprite will need to show itself at the right time, shown below. Add them to your sprite now.

9 Shift + click (in Scratch 2.0) or right-click (in Scratch 1.4) your wall sprite in the Sprite List and duplicate it. Repeat until you have six side wall sprites, including the original.

10 For each of your duplicated wall sprites, you need to change the value of *wall number*. Click each sprite in turn and edit its script. For the first duplicate, change the block **set wall number to 1**, making the number 2. Repeat until you have six walls with wall numbers 1 to 6.

11 Each of the wall sprites needs to respond to a different broadcast number too, this time going from 0 to 5. This is going to be harder to change. Go into your first duplicated wall (it should have a wall number of 2). Find the block **when I receive show left 0**. Click the menu in it and choose **new message**. Create the message "show left 1". Repeat with the other sprites. They should all respond to a broadcast number that is one less than their wall number. For example, the last wall is wall number 6, and it responds to "show left 5".

Beware

Take care with the broadcast name "show left 0" and the related names. If you have extra spaces, the game won't work properly.

Testing the walls

We've now added six walls on the left. Let's test them.

1 The player sprite will be where the main game code sits and it's also a good place to put our testing script. Click the button above the Sprite List to add a new sprite from the library in Scratch 2.0 or from a file in Scratch 1.4. In Scratch 2.0, choose Alex. In Scratch 1.4, pick breakdancer-1. Both are in the People folder.

2 Make a variable called *loop* (for all sprites).

3 Clear the box beside *loop* in the Blocks Palette.

4 Click the player sprite in the Sprite List and add this script to it. It sets *loop* to 5, and uses the **join** block to put it on the end of the words "show left". This is then broadcast. Each time the script repeats, the value of *loop* is one less than before. So the script will broadcast "show left 5", "show left 4" and so on down to zero. It also includes broadcasts for the right walls, ready for when we add them later.

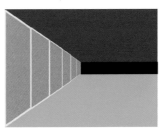

5 Click the **green flag** and you should see something like this picture, although the lines are a bit jagged in Scratch 1.4. If not, check your scripts and lists.

Don't forget

The broadcast "place walls" tells the walls to go to their positions on the Stage. Once positioned, they'll stay there for the whole game, but sometimes they will be hidden.

Beware

In your join block, you need to include a space after "show left" because the broadcasts "show left5" and "show left 5" aren't the same thing. The same applies to the "show right" broadcasts.

Hot tip

The first wall on the left shows itself when it receives "show left 0", the next one when it gets "show left 1", and so on.

Adding the right walls

Next, we need to add the walls on the right to our project. This is a little bit fiddly, but you can reuse a lot of the work you've done already with the walls on the left.

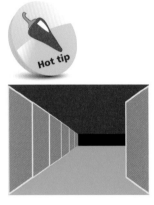

 1 Shift + click or right-click your first side wall sprite in the Sprite List and duplicate it. Your new sprite is called wall7 in Scratch 2.0 and Sprite11 in Scratch 1.4. Look at its code and you should find it uses the wall number of 1.

2 The walls on the right are the same size as those on the left, but they're on the opposite side of the screen. That means we need to change their x position and rotate them (point them in the opposite direction). Drag the **item wall number of wall positions** blocks out of your **go to x: y:** block and keep them in the Scripts Area. Drag a - (minus) operator block into the x hole. Type 0 into the left of it, and then drag your list block back in to the right of it. Add a **point in direction 90** block and change the number in it to **-90**. Your code should look like this:

```
when I receive place walls ▼
set wall number ▼ to 1
go to x: 0 - item wall number of wall positions ▼  y: 0
set size to item wall number of wall sizes ▼ %
point in direction -90▼
```

3 The right walls need to respond to different broadcast names too. They have the same numbers as those on the left (going from 0 to 5), but they are named "show right 0" and so on. Find the block **when I receive show left 0**. Click the menu in it and choose **new message**, and then create the message "show right 0".

4 Repeat this entire process with your other left wall sprites, duplicating them, adjusting their positions and directions and changing the broadcasts they respond to.

Building the test maze

The goal of the test maze is to make it possible to see all the possible viewpoints in the maze, including:

- A long corridor (as you walk down them, the distance to the end reduces, so you don't especially need short corridors)

- A right turn in a side wall

- A left turn in a side wall

- A right turn at the end of a corridor

- A left turn at the end of a corridor

- A dead end

- A T junction, where players must go left or right (or back)

- An exit

In this maze game, a space on the map either contains a wall or a space the player can stand in. You can make the map using graph paper, or by filling in the cells in a spreadsheet, as I have. In the game code, a # sign is used for a wall, an = sign for an empty space, and X for the exit, as shown on the alternative map below:

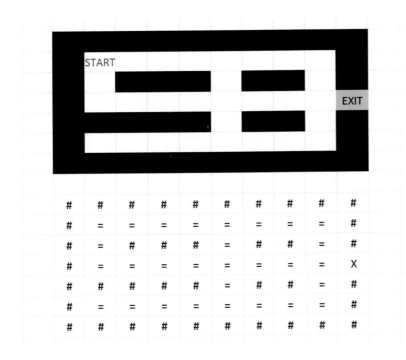

Hot tip

You can use a simple maze to test all these possibilities because players can approach the same corner or turn from different directions.

Hot tip

Why use an equals sign for empty spaces? Because it's visible and roughly the same width as a # sign, unlike a space. When you're entering the code, it makes it easier to enter the map without making mistakes, because you can see how many empty spaces there are, and they will line up with the surrounding walls in the code.

...cont'd

Hot tip

Check your maze data looks right. Each line should be the same length.

Each line of the maze is represented using a string of letters, where # means there's a wall, and = means there's a space. For example, the third line in our maze would be "#=###=##=#". Check it against the map, and remember the first line is the top wall. The lines of the maze are stored in a list. Let's set up the maze now.

1. Click the button above the Sprite List to add a sprite. Later on, you will use it to create maze data from pictures, but for now, it'll just set up the text list we'll be using. I've chosen the same Flower sprite in Scratch 2.0 and tennisball from Scratch 1.4 that I used to generate a maze in the previous maze maker project.

2. Click the **Data** or **Variables** button above the Blocks Palette and click the button to **Make a List**. Call it *maze* and leave the option selected for all sprites. Untick or uncheck the box beside its name in the Blocks Palette to hide it on the Stage.

3. Add the script shown below to your new sprite. You'll need to click the menu in the **when I receive** block to make a new message called "build maze". Use the **delete 1 of maze** block and use the menu to change the 1 to "all".

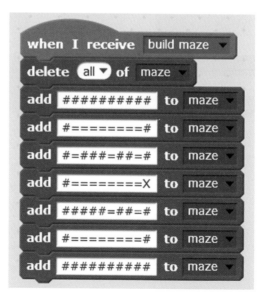

Beware

If you make a mistake when entering your hand-designed mazes, they might be impossible! It doesn't matter so much for our test maze, but it will matter later on when you build more complex mazes.

Entering movement data

The player moves by using the left and right arrow keys to turn on the spot, and using the up and down arrow keys to move forwards or backwards in the direction they are facing.

This means working out the player's movements is a bit trickier than you might expect. The player's position in the maze will be stored in the variables *player x* and *player y*, and the player's direction will be in the variable *player dir*. If you're facing north or south and move forwards, your y position changes. If you're facing west or east, your x position is affected.

Here's a table that shows how the player's position is changed by moving forward in each of the directions:

	Name	player dir	x change	y change
↑	North	1	0	-1
→	East	2	1	0
↓	South	3	0	1
←	West	4	-1	0

For example, imagine the player is in the top left corner, where *player x* is 2 and *player y* is 2. This is the start position in our test map. If the player's direction is 2, the player is facing east. When the player moves forward, the game will add 1 to *player x* and nothing to *player y*, putting the player at position *player x* =3 and *player y* = 2.

If the player is in the same starting position, but turns to face south and moves, their position is changed by adding 1 to their y position, but this does not change their x position.

This table will also be used to work out what the player can see in the maze, based on the direction they are looking towards.

123

Hot tip

The player can move in four directions through the maze. Diagonal movement is not allowed.

Don't forget

The x position is where the player is in the east-west direction, or left-right direction as you view the map. The y position is where the player is in the north-south direction, or up-down direction on the map.

Don't forget

You can often test how a program works on paper. Try using the maze map and this table to simulate some movements to see how it works.

...cont'd

As we did for the wall positions, we'll enter the movement list data into Scratch directly. Follow these steps:

1. We'll store the movement information in two lists called *move x* and *move y*. Click the **Data** or **Variables** button above the Blocks Palette and click the **Make a List** button. Make a list called *move x* for all sprites, and then repeat for *move y*.

> **Make a List**

2. Arrange the list boxes on the Stage so you can see them clearly. Click the + button in the bottom of the *move x* box and in Scratch 1.4, click the orange entry box. Add the numbers shown at the bottom of this page. You can press Enter after each one to move to the next line.

3. Add the data to your *move y* box too, as shown below.

4. We'll also use a list to store the positions the player sprite can be rotated in, which are left and right. Make a list called *facing directions* and enter two numbers into it: -90 and 90.

5. Untick or uncheck the boxes beside your list names in the Blocks Palette to clear the data entry boxes from the Stage. You don't need to see them any more.

move x		**move y**		**facing directions**	
1	0	1	-1	1	-90
2	1	2	0	2	90
3	0	3	1		
4	-1	4	0		
+	length: 4	+	length: 4	+	length: 2

Adding the player scripts

The player sprite, which you added previously for testing, is used for the player display and movement. It also coordinates setting things up at the start of the game.

1 Click the player sprite in the Sprite List. Delete the test script starting with **when green flag clicked** by clicking and dragging it into the Blocks Palette.

2 Click the **Data** or **Variables** button above the Blocks Palette and make three new variables for all sprites: *player x*, *player y* and *player dir*.

3 If you're using Scratch 1.4, there is no block to set the rotation style. Instead, click the tiny left-right arrow button to the left of your sprite, above the Scripts Area.

4 Add the scripts on this page to your player sprite. You should find that four of the broadcasts are already in the menu. You'll need to add new messages for "show walls" and "show player". In Scratch 1.4, the **item random of [list name]** block is called **item any of [list name]**.

The *show player* script is used to position the player and change the player's direction randomly.

The *player to front* script moves the player in front of all other sprites. It's used to stop chunks of wall appearing to be on top of the player, which looks weird.

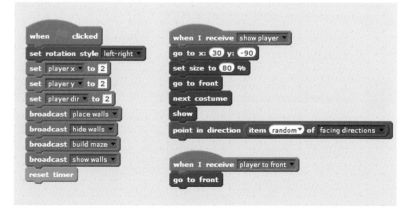

An algorithm is a set of step-by-step instructions to do something, such as draw a maze.

I've distorted the perspective to fit in six layers of depth. In longer corridors this becomes more noticeable, but it means I can enable players to see more movement options into the distance.

Below: The second wall on the right is missing, so the flat front panel of the third wall can be seen. On the left, all of the walls are in place, so the front panels are all hidden.

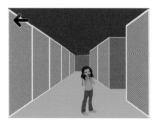

Drawing the maze

Before we make the script to draw the maze, let me tell you how the algorithm works. The game takes the following steps:

 Work out how far the player can see. The script does this by starting at the player's position and moving in the direction the player is looking until it finds a wall or an exit. The program keeps a count of how many steps it took to get there, and remembers this in the variable *depth to show*. The variables *test x*, *test y* and *test dir* are used to remember where the program has got to when looking around the maze for walls.

 All the side walls and the wall in front of the player are hidden.

3 If the *depth to show* is 6 or less, that means the wall in front of the player is within the visible distance. In that case, the front wall sprite is used to show that wall at the right size. Anything further away is in shadow.

4 The program starts in the distance and works its way backwards up the corridor to where the player is standing.

5 With each step, it checks whether there is a wall on the right. It does this by facing the player's direction, and then turning right, moving forward one step and looking to see if that puts it inside a wall. If so, it sends a broadcast to make that wall show itself.

6 For each step, it does the same for the walls on the left, this time turning left and moving forward to check for a wall.

 The walls are drawn from the furthest to the nearest. That means the flat front panel of a wall is hidden if there's another wall joined to it nearer to the player. If there isn't, this front panel is visible, and shows the side turning the player can go down. See the screenshot on the left for an example of what this looks like.

We're ready to start making the scripts that will draw the maze.

1 Add a new sprite to your project. I'm using the pencil sprite in Scratch 2.0 so I can easily remember which one is drawing the maze. In Scratch 1.4, I used the drawing pencil sprite and deleted its script.

2 Click the **Data** or **Variables** button and make these variables for all sprites: *depth to show*, *test x*, *test y*, *character*. Hide them all on the Stage, except for *depth to show*.

3 On your new sprite, create the script below. The character variable should be set to nothing (just delete the 0 in the box). Take care not to add any spaces or other characters in the = blocks, around the X and # symbols. When you fill the diamond hole in the **repeat until** block, add an **or** block first, then two = blocks, and then the **character** blocks. When you set the character to the letter in the maze, start with the **set character to 0** block, then add a **letter 1 of world** block. Put the **item 1 of [list name]** block in, then add the **test x** and **test y** blocks.

Beware

Take care to choose the right variable and list names in the orange and red block menus. At this point in the project, it doesn't appear to do much, and it'll be a while before you can test things. Be careful not to introduce any bugs, because it might take a while to trace them back and fix them.

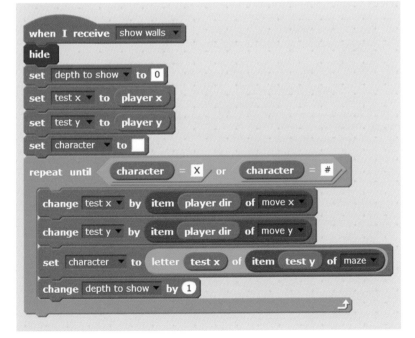

Above: The pencil sprite from Scratch 2.0 that I'm using to draw my maze.

...cont'd

4 The script so far works out how far the player can see. It starts by setting the test variables to the player's position. It then moves one step forwards, using the *move x* and *move y* lists to work out how to change the x and y position for each step, depending on the player's direction. It sets the *character* variable to the symbol at that point on the map, by taking the correct row from the *maze* list (based on the y position) and the correct character from that row (based on the x position). It changes the *depth to show* variable by 1 and repeats until it hits the exit (X) or a wall (#). To test it's working, click the **green flag** and look at the value of *depth to show* on the Stage. If you're using the same map as me and the same character position and direction, it should be 8.

5 Complete your script by adding the blocks below, underneath your **repeat until** block. You'll need to scroll to the bottom of the broadcast menu to make new broadcast messages for "draw front wall", "show right walls", "show left walls", and "show arrow".

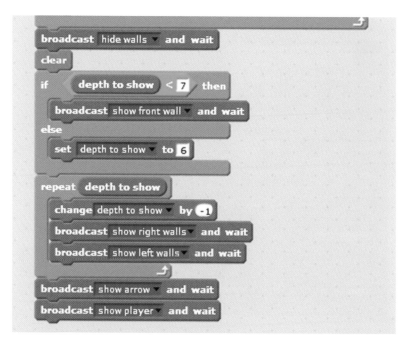

Showing the walls

Let's add the script to show the right walls on the same sprite.

1 Click the **Data** or **Variables** button above the Blocks Palette and make a new variable called *test dir* for all sprites. This is used when the program turns to the right to look for a wall there.

2 Add the script below to your sprite. In the blocks that set the values of *test x* and *test y*, drag in the blocks in this order: **+**, *****, **item 1 of [list]**, **player x** or **player y**, **player dir**, **depth to show**. In the second **if** block, add the **or** block, then the two **=** blocks on each side, then the **character** blocks. Remember to change the list names. You'll need to scroll to the bottom of the menu in the **broadcast and wait** block to add the new message of "show door right".

3 Click the **green flag** to test your game so far. If you're using the same map as me, and it's working, you'll see the right walls appear from the game's start position.

Beware

With all these scripts, take care with all the similar variable, list and broadcast names. If you use the wrong ones, it won't work!

Beware

In your broadcast "show right", add a space after the word "right". Joined with the "depth to show" variable, it will send a message like "show right 1" or "show right 4", which your walls are waiting to receive.

Below: The right walls appear!

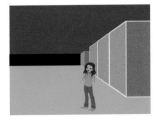

```
when I receive  show right walls ▼

set  test x ▼  to  ( player x  +  ( item  ( player dir )  of  move x ▼  *  depth to show ) )

set  test y ▼  to  ( player y  +  ( item  ( player dir )  of  move y ▼  *  depth to show ) )

set  test dir ▼  to  ( player dir  +  1 )

if  ( test dir  =  5 )  then
    set  test dir ▼  to  1

change  test x ▼  by  ( item  ( test dir )  of  move x ▼ )

change  test y ▼  by  ( item  ( test dir )  of  move y ▼ )

set  character ▼  to  ( letter  ( test x )  of  ( item  ( test y )  of  maze ▼ ) )

if  (( character  =  X )  or  ( character  =  # ))  then
    broadcast  ( join  show right  depth to show )  and wait

if  ( character  =  X )  then
    broadcast  show door right ▼  and wait
```

...cont'd

There's also a script for showing the left walls.

1 Shift + click or right-click the script for "show right walls" that you just made, and duplicate it.

2 In the **when I receive** block at the top, click the menu and choose "show left walls".

3 In the **set test dir to player dir + 1** block, swap the plus block for a minus block, and make it read **set test dir to player dir - 1**.

4 In the **if test dir = 5** block, change the 5 to 0. In the **set test dir block** inside its bracket, change the 1 to 4.

5 In the **broadcast and wait** block, change "show right" to "show left" (and remember to keep the space after "left"). Change "show door right" to "show door left". Your final script is shown below:

Don't forget

The brown broadcast and receive blocks are yellow Control blocks in Scratch 1.4.

Below: Click the green flag, and it should look something like this!

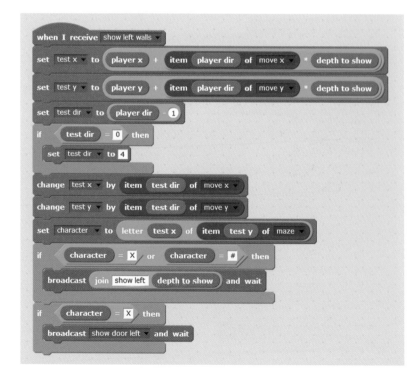

130

The drawing sprite also triggers the script to draw the wall in front of the player.

1 Click the **front wall** in the Sprite List. You have so many sprites now that you might need to use the scrollbar at the side of the Sprite List from time to time to find the one you want. Add the scripts below to it. For the **change x by** blocks, add the blocks in this order: *****, **/**, **item 1 of wall sizes**, **+**, **depth to show**.

2 Show the *depth to show* variable on the Stage and double-click its box on the Stage until the slider appears. Click and slide it left and right to change the variable's value to a number between 1 and 6. Click the **clear** block in the Blocks Palette and click your new script. You should see the front wall drawn at different distances. It won't join up with the side walls properly yet. The side walls need to be drawn on top of this front wall.

Hot tip

In Scratch 2.0, you can click the **i** button on a sprite in the Sprite List, and then choose "show" to show it on the Stage. You could use this to show one or two of the side walls so you can see how they join to the front wall.

Don't forget

You show a variable on the Stage by ticking the box beside its name in the Data or Variables part of the Blocks Palette.

Below: The front wall. Normally the side walls cover part of it.

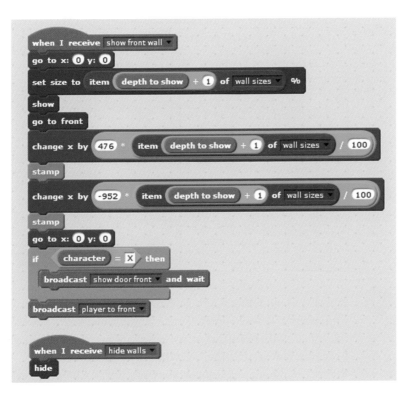

131

Hot tip

Professional game designers usually test their programs as they build them, just like we are, so that they can fix any bugs before they become too hard to find.

Hot tip

As you build this program, and others, try to understand how it works. If you think about what the blocks do, rather than just copying them, you're much less likely to make a mistake.

Hot tip

To tidy up the Stage, clear the boxes beside all the variables and list names. They're in the Data or Variables part of the Blocks Palette.

Testing the maze display

You can now take a tour around your test maze. We haven't added the player's movement controls yet, but you can edit the code to put the player in any starting position and then view the maze from there.

1 Click your player sprite in the Sprite List and find the script starting with **when green flag clicked**.

2 Change the values for *player x* to 6, *player y* to 2 and *player dir* to 3 (south). Click the green flag and the Stage should look like the picture on the right. Take a look at the map earlier in this chapter, and check it makes sense to you.

3 Use the table below to change the player's starting position and direction to other viewpoints, and check they make sense. Try some others of your own too.

player x	player y	player dir	viewpoint
9	6	1	
4	4	4	
8	6	2	

4 If you find something isn't working as you expect, check your scripts. If walls don't appear when they should, check the broadcast names they're looking out for in their **when I receive** blocks, and their *wall numbers*. If the script shows the wrong view, check your *move x* and *move y* lists.

Adding player movement

To make testing easier, and to start adding the game into our maze, we can add the player movement controls.

1 Click your player sprite in the Sprite List.

2 Add the script below to your sprite. Use the **when space key pressed** block and use the menu to change the key to the left arrow. This block is an Events block in Scratch 2.0 and a Control block in Scratch 1.4.

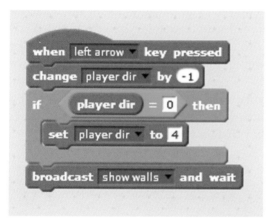

Hot tip

You can test it works already by clicking the Stage and then pressing the left and right keys to rotate your player.

133

3 Shift + click or right-click your script to duplicate it, and change it for the right key movement. You need to change the key detected and the numbers in the three white boxes, to make the script below.

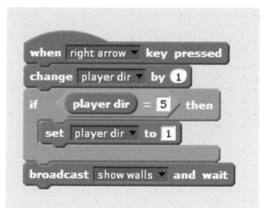

Hot tip

These scripts change the player direction variable, either increasing it or decreasing it. If the direction becomes too small (there is no direction 0), it's reset to 4, which is the direction the player should face if they turn left from direction 1. A similar idea is used for turning right, but with different numbers.

...cont'd

Hot tip

The messages in the **broadcast** and **when I receive** blocks are sorted alphabetically.

Don't forget

Whenever you make a variable, you can hide it on the Stage (unless the instructions say you need it for testing or for players to see). Clear the boxes beside the variable names in the Blocks Palette to hide them.

Beware

When playing the game, don't tap the keys too quickly. Give the screen time to refresh between each move.

4 Click the **Data** or **Variables** button and create two new variables, called *old player x* and *old player y* for all sprites. Clear their boxes in the Blocks Palette to hide them.

5 Add the script below to your player sprite. When you come to the green operator blocks, add the = block first, then the **letter 1 of world** block into the left of it, then the **item 1 of [list name]** block into the right of it. Finally, add the **player x** and **player y** blocks. You'll need to make a new broadcast message for "game completed". This script uses an idea you'll often see in games: we remember the player's position (using the *old player x* and *old player y* variables), then we do the move they want. If that puts them somewhere they can't be (in a wall), we move them straight back to where they were before, by changing their position variables back to their old values.

6 Now you can walk around your maze using the left and right keys to turn, and up arrow to move forwards. Try it!

7 The game feels much smoother with the ability to walk backwards as well. It saves players having to turn twice if they change their mind and want to go back a step, perhaps explore an intriguing corridor after all. Add the script below to your player sprite to enable players to use the down key to move backwards. It reuses the *test dir* variable to remember the direction the player is walking when they go backwards. It's the player's direction number, plus 2, and with 4 taken off if that makes the number greater than 4. Take another look at the table of direction numbers earlier in this chapter if you're not sure.

8 Test it works by moving backwards and forwards. Make sure you can't walk backwards or forwards through walls.

You might encounter a bug if you walk through the door. Although you can't see it, it's in the map and we haven't taught the program how to handle it yet.

135

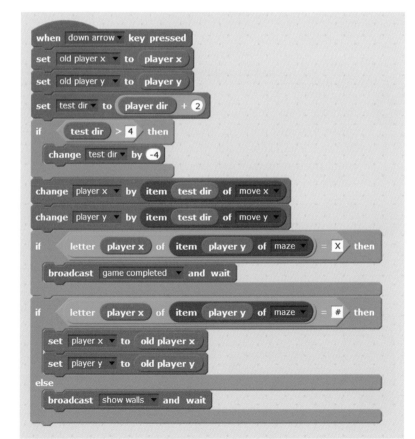

Hot tip

You can save some time here by duplicating and editing the script for moving forwards, but be careful not to miss any differences.

Beware

Take care to use the *player*, *old player* and *test dir* variables in the right place.

Adding a compass

The maze can be confusing, so let's give the player a compass.

1 In **Scratch 2.0**, click the button above the Sprite List to add a new sprite from the library. Choose Arrow2 from the Things folder. Click the **Costumes** tab. Click the Up costume and drag it to the top of your costumes list. Click the right costume, and drag it to the bottom. The end result should look like the picture on the right.

2 In **Scratch 1.4**, click the button to draw a sprite above the Sprite List. Paint an up arrow and click **OK**. Click the **Costumes** tab, and then click the **Copy** button. Click the button to **Edit** your new costume, and rotate it. Add a total of three costumes for the other three directions, in the order shown here.

3 Add the scripts below to your arrow sprite. You will find the "show arrow" message is already in the menu, but you'll need to make new messages for "show map" and "show landscape".

4 Turn in the maze to test the compass. It always points towards north, so if it's facing left and you turn left, it should point up.

New costume:

1 arrow2-d
46x55

2 arrow2-b
55x46

3 arrow2-c
46x55

4 arrow2-a
55x46

Hot tip

You should end up with one sprite that has four arrow costumes, in the order shown on this page.

Hot tip

The controls to rotate the image in Scratch 1.4 look like this. They're in the top left of the Paint Editor.

Hot tip

The "show landscape" and "show map" broadcasts aren't used anywhere else yet. Later on, they'll be used when we turn visual maps into a maze list, and when the game completion sequence is shown. We want to hide the arrow at both of those times.

```
when I receive show arrow
go to x: -200 y: 140
switch costume to player dir
go to front
show
```

```
when I receive show map
hide
```

```
when I receive show landscape
hide
```

Adding the exit door

Let's give the player a chance to escape!

 1 You previously added your door sprite to your project. Click it in the Sprite List to choose it.

 2 Add the script to the right to your door sprite.

3 Click the **Data** or **Variables** button above the Blocks Palette and make a new variable, called *door position*. It can be for all sprites. It will be used to remember the depth at which the door should be shown.

4 Add the script below to your door sprite. It uses the lists you've already set up for the wall positions and wall sizes, to put the door in the right place and change its size to match the wall it's on. You should find the broadcast messages you need are already set up. In the **go to x: y:** block, add the blocks in this order: *****, **/**, **item 1 of wall sizes**, **door position**. Use a similar order for the **change y** block.

Below: The exit door viewed from three different points. Also shown is the compass in the top left.

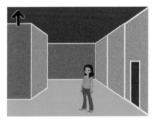

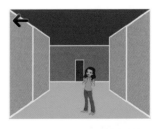

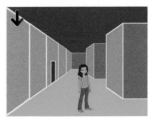

...cont'd

Subtracting the door's x position from 0 (the middle of the screen) puts it on the other half of the screen.

Beware

When you duplicate a script, you also copy any errors in it! If you make a mistake in one of the left or right door scripts, remember to check the other one too.

Hot tip

In Chapter Nine, we'll add a completion sequence and some other cool game features.

5 Make the script below. If you're careful, you can copy the left door script and edit it. The changes are in the **when I receive**, **switch costume**, **go to x: y:** and **change x** blocks.

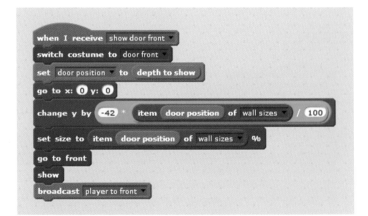

6 Add the script below to show the front door.

7 Test it works! Find your door in the maze and walk towards it with it in front, to the left and to the right of you.

9 3D Maze Explorer: Finishing touches

You can easily make a perfect filled circle by setting the line width in the costumes editor to large, and clicking once with the Paintbrush tool to draw a spot.

Don't forget

There is no **set rotation style** block in Scratch 1.4. Leave it out of the script. Above the Costumes Area, click the double-headed arrow beside the small butterfly sprite to make it only face left-right.

Rewarding the player

After players have fought their way through your fiendish maze, it's only fair to give them a reward. Here's how to make a game completion sequence that makes them feel it was all worthwhile.

1 Click the button above the Blocks Palette to draw a new sprite. Create a picture of the outside world.

2 Add the scripts shown below to the new sprite you've created.

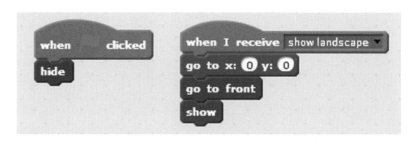

3 In **Scratch 2.0**, click the button above the Sprite List to add a sprite from the library. Add Butterfly1.

4 In **Scratch 1.4**, click the button above the Sprite List to add a sprite from the library. Add butterfly1-a. Click the **Costumes** tab, and click the **Import** button. Add the costume butterfly1-b. You should have one butterfly sprite with two costumes.

5 Add the script on the right to your butterfly.

6 Click the **Data** or **Variables** button and make new variables called *score* and *finish time* for all sprites. Untick or uncheck the boxes to hide them from the Stage.

7 Click your player sprite in the Sprite List and give it this script. You should find all the broadcasts are in the menu already. Make sure you put a space before the word "seconds" in the **join** block.

```
when I receive  game completed
set  finish time  to  timer
clear
broadcast  hide walls  and wait
broadcast  show landscape  and wait
broadcast  show butterfly
go to front
show
say  Freedom at last!  for  2  secs
say  It took you...  for  2  secs
say  join  finish time  seconds  for  2  secs
say  join  Items collected:  score  for  2  secs
```

8 Test your game. You should now be able to fully explore your maze and escape!

Hot tip

You could add some celebratory music to the script on this page. You can download some tunes for your Scratch projects from the Cool Scratch Projects in easy steps part of my website.

141

Don't forget

The **timer** block is a Sensing block.

Left: The game completion sequence, featuring my landscape design, an animated butterfly and a happy escapee. Ah! You can almost feel the fresh air!

Hot tip

With some sprites it can be hard for players to judge how far away they are. These food sprites work well because they look like they're sitting on the ground.

Beware

You can have multiple prizes in the game, but should position them so that the player can only see one at a time. Otherwise the front wall will sometimes cover bits of the prize.

Hot tip

I'm calling the objects in the maze prizes, because it's a bit more flexible than calling them food. If you later on change them to keys or magic spells, it'll still make sense if the scripts talk about prizes.

Adding collectables

You can make your 3D Maze Explorer game more fun by hiding things in the maze for players to search for. I'll show you how to add a cake in Scratch 2.0, and a bowl of cheesy puffs in Scratch 1.4. If you add other objects later, you might need to adjust the center of the costume so they don't look like they're hovering.

1 Click your maze building sprite, the flower or tennisball. Find the script that creates the list for the maze. Replace the = sign with a C character where you'd like your collectable to be. You can add a few if you'd like to.

```
when I receive build maze ▼
hide
delete all ▼ of maze ▼
add ######### to maze ▼
add #=======# to maze ▼
add #=###=##=# to maze ▼
add #====C===X to maze ▼
add #####=##=# to maze ▼
add #=C======# to maze ▼
add ######### to maze ▼
```

2 Go to your sprite that displays your maze, which is the pencil sprite. Add the script below to it. For the **set test x to** and **set test y to** blocks, add the blocks in this order: **+**, *****, **item 1 of list**, **player x** or **player y**, **player dir**, **depth to show**. For the **set character to** block, add the **letter 1 of world** block, then the **item 1 of list** block, followed by the **test x** and **test y** blocks. You'll need to make new messages for "prize is in view" and "show prize".

```
when I receive show prize ▼
set test x ▼ to (player x) + (item (player dir) of move x ▼) * (depth to show)
set test y ▼ to (player y) + (item (player dir) of move y ▼) * (depth to show)
set character ▼ to letter (test x) of (item (test y) of maze ▼)
if character = C then
    broadcast prize is in view ▼ and wait
```

3 Also on the sprite that displays your maze, find your script that begins with the **when I receive show walls** block. In the **repeat depth to show** bracket, there are broadcasts for **show right walls and wait** and **show left walls and wait**. Add a new block after them to **broadcast show prize and wait**.

4 Click the **Data** or **Variables** button and make a new variable called *prize depth* for all sprites. Make a list called *prize positions* for all sprites. Click the + button in the list's box on the Stage and add these numbers: -122, -81, -54, -34, -23, -17. Clear the boxes beside the new variable and list in the Blocks Palette.

5 Click the button above the Sprite List to add a new sprite from the library. In Scratch 2.0, choose the cake sprite and in Scratch 1.4, choose the cheesy puffs.

6 Add the scripts below to your cake or cheesy puffs sprite. Click the green flag and walk around your maze to test the prize appears.

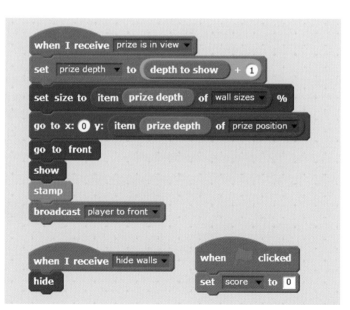

Hot tip

I found the y positions for the objects by experimentation. If you add other objects, you might need to adjust their y positions in this list to make them look like they're in the right position on the floor.

Hot tip

The prize position numbers are the y positions of where the prize will appear at each level of depth. The x position is always 0, in the middle of the screen.

Below: A cake at the crossroads.

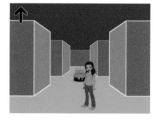

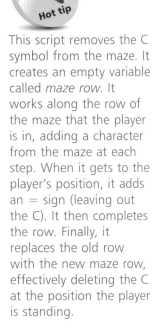

Collecting items

Let's give the player the ability to pick up items.

 1 Go to your player sprite. Find the script that starts with a **when up arrow key pressed** block. Add the blocks below to the end of that script, starting with the **if** block. You'll need to make a new message for the broadcast.

2 Right-click or Shift + click the blocks you added and duplicate them. Join them onto the end of your script that starts with a **when down arrow key pressed** block.

3 Make a new variable for all sprites called *maze row* and clear its box in the Blocks Palette to hide it on the Stage.

4 Add the script below to your player sprite.

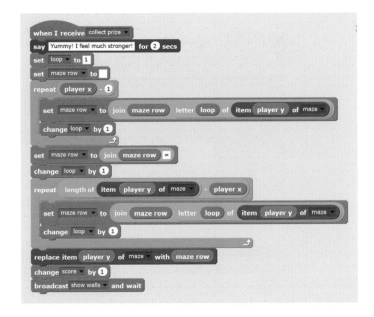

Using drawn mazes

You can manually design your maze using graph paper or a spreadsheet, and then enter the information into the maze list. But you can also design your mazes on screen and use a script to turn your images into the text format this game uses.

1 Find a maze image. This can be a randomly generated maze that you saved from the previous project, or a maze you made by editing the grid from that project. You can use a white pen to wipe out the walls. Don't worry about removing every trace of them: a good chunk out of the middle will do. The player starts in the top left and the exit will be in the bottom right, so make sure that makes sense in your maze design. Use the whole grid.

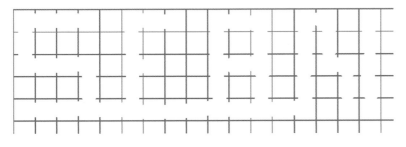

2 In your 3D maze game, click the button to add a new sprite from a file. Choose your maze image. Add the scripts on the right to this sprite. Make a new message for "hide map".

3 Go to your **player** sprite. Find the **when green flag clicked** script, and change the starting values of both *player x* and *player y* to 2.

4 Make two new variables called *builder x* and *builder y*, for all sprites. Clear their boxes (and any other variables or lists) in the Blocks Palette to hide them on the Stage.

Hot tip

You can download some maze images and a blank grid at **www. ineasysteps.com** or the author's website, **www.sean.co.uk**

Hot tip

The maze maker program can add "components" at a dead end. The 3D maze works better if you don't put anything there. If you included that feature, you can turn it off by taking the **stamp** block out of your maze maker project. It's on the cat sprite, in the "when green flag clicked" script.

Hot tip

This script doesn't include the ability to use collectables. Perhaps you could add that, using a different color in your maze image?

Hot tip

For the **set maze row to** block, drag in a **set maze row to 0** block and delete the 0 in it. The **touching color** block needs to match the color of the walls in your maze image.

Don't forget

When you start the game, there will be a short delay while the maze is compiled. You can use it to study the map! If you want to see what's going on, replace the **hide** block on this page with a **show** block, and add a **hide** block at the end of the script.

Beware

Take special care with the yellow brackets here, and with what belongs inside each one. This is a tricky script to build!

...cont'd

5 Go to your **maze builder** sprite (flower or tennisball). Find the script that starts with **when I receive build maze**. Keep the **when I receive build maze, hide,** and **delete all of maze** blocks. Drag the rest away from the script. Complete your script as shown below:

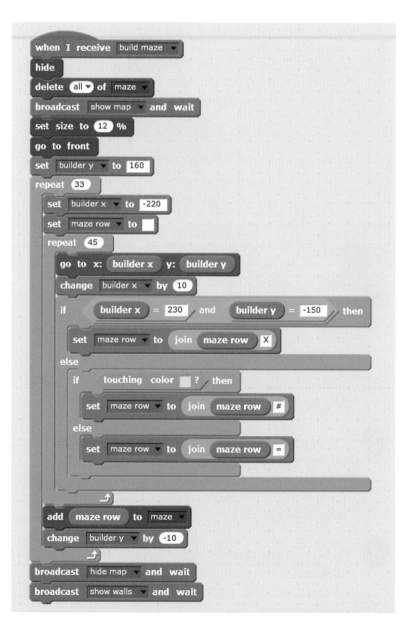

Adding a map

It's not easy navigating the maze, but you can add an optional map feature if you've used an image to generate your maze.

 1 Add the script below to your player sprite. It shows the map when you press the M key, and waits until you press space before hiding it again.

```
when m ▾ key pressed
broadcast in game map ▾ and wait
wait until key space ▾ pressed?
broadcast hide map ▾
broadcast show walls ▾
```

```
when I receive show map ▾
hide
```

 2 Add the script below to your maze image sprite. It hides the maze, shows the map, and plots the player's position on the map as a purple spot.

```
when I receive in game map ▾
clear
broadcast hide walls ▾ and wait
broadcast show map ▾ and wait
stamp
hide
set size to 5 %
set pen color to ▮
set pen size to 8
pen up
go to x: -230 + player x * 10 y: 170 - player y * 10
pen down
move 1 steps
```

Below: A close-up of the map, showing the player's position.

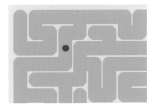

Don't forget

Make sure your player starts in a sensible place. In my scripts, I've assumed you're making a rectangular maze. Other shapes are possible, but make sure your player begins the game inside the maze, not outside it!

Customizing the game

Congratulations on building this project! Now you can customize the game with your own ideas.

- **Your own maze layout.** It doesn't have to follow the rules of my randomly generated mazes. You could have loops, spell out words and all kinds of things. For best results, keep corridors shorter than 6 steps long. The exit should go on an edge wall, but it can go on any edge of the maze. If you want to include objects to pick up, it's easiest to enter the maze list as text. Image mazes don't feature objects.

- **Monsters!** Perhaps you could put some monsters in some dead ends of your maze that end the game if the player walks into them, or put them in the path but allow the player to zap them so they can still complete the maze. Hint: use a new letter to represent monsters in the *maze* list.

- **Add keys.** Perhaps you can keep track of how many items the player picks up in your maze. You could make them keys and only let players through the door if their score shows they've collected enough.

- **Add sound effects.** How about some cheering sound effects or music when the player escapes? Or walking sounds?

- **Adding collectables to mazes made from images.** You need to make sure the player can only see one collectable at a time, because there's only one prize sprite. You might find bits of wall overlap the prize if the player can see more than one prize at a time. The simplest solution is to add prizes to the four corners of the maze, but you could add them in random locations and make sure they're not too close. Be careful not to replace a wall with a cake!

- **Multiple mazes.** You could include several mazes in the game and have one randomly chosen at the start of each game. This is easiest if you use the drawn mazes, add several and set the costume to a random one at the start.

- **Mutating mazes.** When you pick something up, it's replaced with an = sign to leave an empty space. If you replace it with a # it becomes a wall when you move away from that position. Now you can make one-way passages!

10 Sprites, Cameras, Action!

Sprites, Cameras, Action!

The Raspberry Pi Camera Module can take photos for costumes. In this project, you'll use it to make a stop motion studio. Stop motion is an animation technique where you make a film by taking a photo, changing the scene slightly, taking another photo, and repeating. When you play the photos back quickly, it looks like things are moving around. You can have great fun using household objects, Lego minifigures or toys for your films.

These are the keys used in this project:

- **Space.** Shoot a frame and add it to the end of the sequence.

- **Left and right arrow.** Move through the frames you've shot.

- **P.** Play your animation so far.

- **I.** Insert: shoot a frame and add it before the one you're currently looking at.

- **D.** Delete the frame you're looking at.

- **E.** Erase all the frames data. This removes all the data that's used for playing back the frames in the right order.

- **C.** Add a caption (speech bubble) at the point where the mouse cursor is on the current frame.

Beware

This project only works on the Raspberry Pi, using the Raspberry Pi Camera Module. The project works but runs slow on the Model B+. To avoid corrupting your film, wait for each action to finish before you start another one.

Hot tip

The Camera Module is an official Raspberry Pi product and costs about $25 or £20 (*correct at the time of printing*).

Below: I use Lego bricks to mount my camera. The cable is held tight between two long Lego bricks.

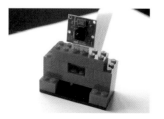

Shooting and viewing shots

Before we can start shooting, we need to set up a few things.

1 Connect your camera to the Raspberry Pi with it switched off. If you look at your Raspberry Pi so that the HDMI socket is on the bottom, there is a plastic connector to the right of the HDMI

socket. Press it at both ends between your finger and thumb, then lift to open it. Insert the cable from your Camera Module, with the silver side facing the HDMI socket. Press the cable to the bottom of the connector, and then press the plastic connector shut again to clamp the cable in place.

Hot tip

If you have a Raspberry Pi Zero, the camera connector is on the right edge of the board. You need a new cable for your camera to connect it. Find more information at **www.raspberrypi.org**

2 Switch your Raspberry Pi on and go into the desktop environment. Click the **Menu** button, click **Preferences**, and then click **Raspberry Pi Configuration**. Click the **Interfaces** tab and enable the camera. Reboot if necessary.

Hot tip

To delete a costume, click the X button beside it in the Costumes Area.

3 Start a new Scratch project. On the cat sprite, click the **Costumes** tab and click the **Paint** button. Design a new costume that fills the Stage, to be the title frame of your animation.

4 In the **Costumes** tab, delete the cat costumes so you're left with only your title slide on the sprite.

5 Click the **Variables** button above the Blocks Palette.

Hot tip

The word "frame" refers to one image in your film sequence.

...cont'd

Hot tip

When you save a project, it also saves all the costumes and list data. So you can save a film by saving the project with a new file name.

Beware

In this chapter, I'm using Scratch 1.4 on the Raspberry Pi, so the blocks will look a bit different to the rest of the book.

Hot tip

It's okay to test the camera with photos of anything. I'll show you how to delete your test shots before you make your film.

6 Make these variables for all sprites: *caption*, *counter*, and *current frame*. Clear the boxes beside them in the Blocks Palette to hide them from the Stage.

7 Make four lists: *caption text*, *caption x*, *caption y* and *frames*. These should also be for all sprites. Clear the boxes beside them in the Blocks Palette. The *caption text*, *caption x* and *caption y* lists are used to remember the caption on a frame, if there is one, and where it is positioned on screen. The *frames* list is used to remember the order we want to play the frames in the animation. This list enables us to insert and delete frames. We can't change the photos or their order in the sprite's costumes once they're taken, but we can change the order we view them in, or even leave some out, when we play the film.

8 Add the script below to your sprite:

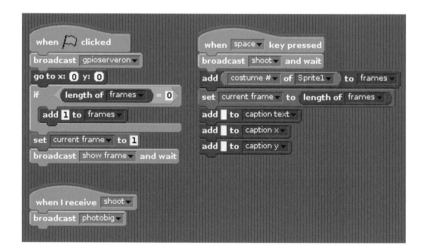

9 Click the **green flag** and tap the space bar. A light flashes on your camera, and then the Stage will fill with a photo from your camera. Click the **Costumes** tab, and you should see a photo has been added from the camera as a costume. It might take a moment, so be patient.

10 Add the script below to your sprite. This one shows the relevant frame when browsing the shots or playing the film back. We use the frames list to work out which costume (or photo) to show for the current frame.

Hot tip

The animation works best if you only make quite small changes to the scene before taking each photo. For example, you might move an arm a little bit, or move a figure a small step forward. It might take a lot of shots to move from one side of the Stage to another, but it will look smoother when you play the film.

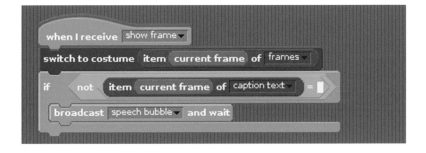

11 Add the scripts below to your sprite.

12 These scripts enable you to browse through the frames using the cursor keys and to play the whole sequence by pressing P. Take a few shots by pressing space and then check you can browse through them and play the film back. You can even make a simple animation now!

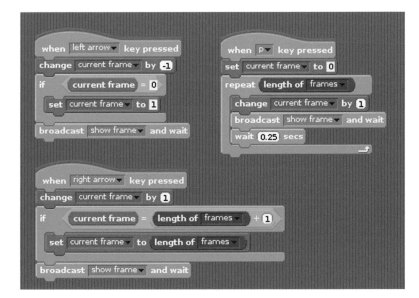

Hot tip

You can buy or make stickers with eyes and mouths on. They help turn any object into a stop motion superstar.

Editing the frame sequence

At the moment, the script works great if you never make a mistake. But what if you want to delete or insert a frame? Let's add some controls for that now.

1 Add this script to your sprite. When you press D, it deletes the frame you're looking at with a fade-out effect.

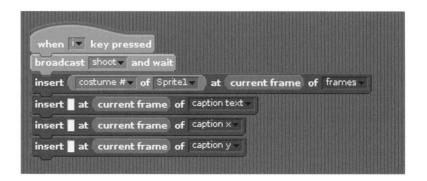

I used a pack of playing cards when testing the script. They made it easy for me to drop a number into the scene so I could tell which order I took the shots in. This was especially helpful when testing the ability to insert and delete frames.

2 Add the script below to your sprite. It will take a new photo and insert it before the one you're looking at.

Photos are always added at the end of the costumes list. Our script to insert a frame inserts the new costume number in the frames list before the current frame. When we play the film, it'll show us the new costume where we inserted it in the list.

3 Use the arrow keys to go through your sequence and try deleting and inserting frames. Press P to play the film or use the arrow keys and check the frames are in the right place, or not shown if you've deleted them.

4 Add a new sprite to your project. It will be used to erase all the frame and caption data. Add the scripts on the right to your sprite.

Hot tip

The script erases the data if you enter "Y" and doesn't erase if you enter anything else. We tell people to enter "N" so they can be sure they know how to keep their data and we can explain it in a few words.

```
when ⚑ clicked
hide

when e▾ key pressed
go to x: 0 y: 0
show
ask Delete all frame data? Enter Y or N and wait
if    answer = Y
    delete all▾ of frames▾
    delete all▾ of caption text▾
    delete all▾ of caption x▾
    delete all▾ of caption y▾
    add 1 to frames▾
    set current frame▾ to 1
    broadcast show frame▾ and wait
hide
```

5 If you're sure you're happy to delete your film data, press E to test the erase function. Try entering N first and then press P to confirm your data is still there. Then try erasing the data properly.

Beware

Before taking a photo, click Sprite1 in the Sprite List. The camera puts photos on the current sprite, even if the script taking the photo is on a different one.

6 There isn't a way to delete costumes using blocks, so after you erase the frames data, click the main sprite, click the **Costumes** tab, and delete all the costumes except the first one by clicking the X button on their right.

Below: The fantasy1-a sprite pops up to make sure you really do want to delete your data.

155

You could adapt the caption script to enable the user to enter the name of sounds to play in each frame. You can use the **play sound** block together with a list item, so you could use a list to store the sounds (if any) that each frame has.

Hot tip

You could add Scratch sprites to your film. Here's a script to show a ghost at frame 5. It doesn't change how long the frame is shown for, so the ghost only flashes briefly unless there's a speech bubble. Perhaps you could use a list to store how long each frame should appear for?

Adding captions

You can use Scratch to add speech bubbles to the characters in your film. Each frame can have one speech bubble. You move the mouse pointer to the character who will speak, before pressing C.

1 Add a new sprite to your project. It's never seen so why not click the ? button above the Sprite List to get a random sprite.

2 Add the scripts on this page to your new sprite. Take particular care to choose the right lists in the list blocks. The sprite is set to 1% to enable the speech bubble to be positioned accurately. The ghost effect is used to make the sprite invisible. Sprites that are hidden don't show their speech bubbles.

3 Test it works. Click the **green flag** and use the arrow keys to move through your frames and try adding some captions. Check they appear when you play back the film using the P key.

11 Super Wheelie in ScratchJr

Introducing ScratchJr

Hot tip

ScratchJr is free. To find it on your device's app store, follow the download links at www.scratchjr.org

ScratchJr (where Jr is short for "junior") is an app for Android tablets and the iPad, designed to introduce younger children to coding. It's great for the rest of us too, because it enables us to make games and interactive stories anywhere, any time.

Because it's designed for younger children, ScratchJr uses very little text. As somebody who's used Scratch, you'll find some ideas are familiar, but you'll also find some things are different or missing. Sprites can only rotate in multiples of 15 degrees, and the Stage is only 20 squares wide by 15 tall, for example. The **forever** block can only be used for an entire script, not for just the last part of it. There are no variables or random numbers, which play a role in many, perhaps most, Scratch games. There is no pen, either. You'll probably spot other differences as you try it.

Don't forget

The Lifelong Kindergarten Group at the MIT Media Lab invented Scratch and helped to make ScratchJr.

You can use six color-coded broadcasts, though, and you also have pages, which are like levels in a game, or scenes in a story. Sprites can react when they touch other sprites (although they can't tell which sprites they touched), and can respond to taps.

The screen layout is shown below. As in Scratch, you have a Stage where your animation or game is played. You have characters (like Scratch's sprites) that you can give commands in the forms of blocks. The blocks are chosen from the Blocks Palette, and joined together in the Programming Area (the same as the Scripts Area in Scratch). On the right is the Pages Area where you manage up to four different pages in your project.

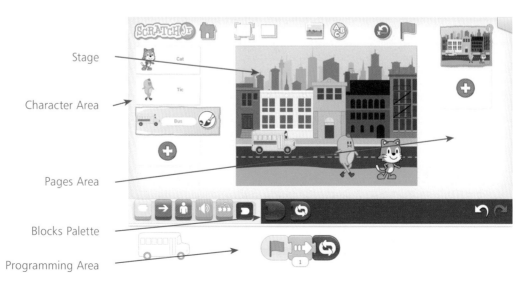

Stage

Character Area

Pages Area

Blocks Palette

Programming Area

Starting Super Wheelie

In this project, I'll show you how to make a game called Super Wheelie. In it, you ride your bike along the beach to get home. You have to do a wheelie to jump over mushrooms, and if you hit one by mistake, you'll bounce off into the sea. After building it, you can customize this game with additional sounds (a splash, perhaps?), an extra level and different hazards to jump.

Hot tip

Tap the Home icon in the top left to go to your projects, then tap the book in the top right for a guide to all the blocks.

1 Tap the ScratchJr icon to start the app. When it opens, tap the Home icon (pictured). Tap the large + button to start a new project.

2 Tap and hold the cat in the Character Area on the left. When the red **delete** button appears, tap it to delete the cat.

3 Tap the background icon in the middle above the Stage. It looks like a picture.

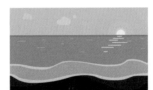

4 Bring in the Beach Sunset background (right). Level 1 takes place at sunset. Level 2, (below) will take place at night.

Hot tip

It's easier to play games in full screen mode, otherwise ScratchJr might think you're trying to move the sprite on the Stage. The **full screen** button is above the Stage on the left. Beside it is a button to turn the grid on or off to help position characters.

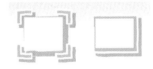

Left: The finished Super Wheelie game with an ace biker in mid-flight.

Hot tip

You can record any sound using the microphone. What other effects could you add?

Beware

Your script won't move on until the sound finishes playing, so I played the recording at the end of the jumping animation.

Hot tip

For best results, start talking as soon as you tap the **record** button, and tap the square **stop** button as soon as you finish.

Building the first level

Now let's add the player's character to the game.

1 Tap the + button in the Character Area and swipe until you find the bike. Tap it twice to add it to your game.

2 Now let's put your face into that image! Tap the Paintbrush button on the bike in the Character Area to enter the Paint Editor. Tap the **camera** button on the right, and then tap the face area. Line up your face, and then tap the camera icon at the bottom. Tap the **tick** button in the top-right corner to finish.

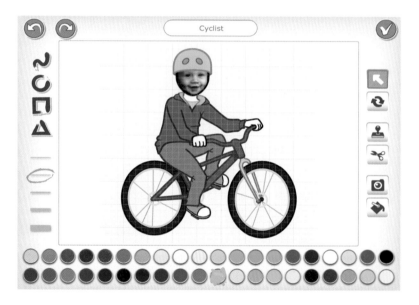

3 Let's add a sound effect to our wheelie. Tap the green speaker icon in the Blocks Palette and tap the dotted microphone icon on its right to record a new sound. Tap the **red circle** button to start recording and say "Wheee!" or something similar. Tap the **square** button when you've finished. Tap the **triangle** to hear what you've done. If it's okay, tap the tick in the top right corner. Otherwise, you can record again.

4 You build scripts in ScratchJr in a similar way as in Scratch. Tap the color-coded button to the left of the Blocks Palette to see the right blocks. Drag them from the Blocks Palette into the Programming Area below. In ScratchJr, blocks are read from left to right, instead of from top to bottom. Start by adding the script below. When the **green flag** is tapped, it sets the sprite to its default size, and then reduces its size by 4. Tap the number in the reduce by 2 block to open the keypad.

Don't forget

Remember to change the numbers in the boxes where necessary so that everything moves the right number of times.

5 Add this script to your bike to code the wheelies. This is what the script does: When the bike is tapped, it tilts to point up, goes up four steps, then tilts back to be level and drops down again. At the end, it plays our recording.

Hot tip

When a character goes off the left of the Stage, it appears on the right of the Stage. That means when the player cycles past one mushroom and it goes off the screen, another one comes into view on the right. Actually, it's the same one!

6 Tap the + button in the Character Area and add the mushroom. Give it this script. The "arrow and x" block puts it in its starting position. The mushroom goes from right to left three times, and gets bigger each time.

Below: Turning left once points the bike towards the sky.

...cont'd

To test the game so far, tap page 1 in the Pages Area and then tap the green flag. Tap the bike to jump.

Don't forget

To delete a character, tap and hold it in the Character Area. To change the background, use the button above the Stage.

Below: Our second page is the animation of bobbing in the sea when the bike crashes.

7 Now let's position our characters. Drag the bike on the Stage to the bottom left. Drag the mushroom to the bottom right, so it's half off the screen.

8 In the Pages Area on the right, tap the + button to add a new page. Delete the cat again, and change the background to the Underwater background.

9 Tap your first page in the Pages Area. Tap the bike in the Character Area and drag it onto your second page in the Pages Area. This copies the bike and its scripts to your new page.

10 Tap the Underwater scene in your Pages Area. Drag the bike's scripts into the Blocks Palette to delete them. Then add this new script:

11 In the Pages Area, tap your first page. Tap the bike in the Character Area and add the script on the right to it. When you add a page to a project, a block to jump to it is added in the red part of the Blocks Palette. This script is triggered when the character touches another character (the mushroom) and moves the game to page two, the crash animation.

Adding the second level

Let's add level 2 as a new page. This time, there are two mushrooms to jump, and you arrive at your house after leaping three pairs of them.

 1 Tap the + button in the Pages Area to add a new page. Delete the cat as you did before.

2 Tap the background icon above the Stage and add the Beach Night background.

3 Tap the first page in the Pages Area, to get to level 1 of the game. Drag both characters, the bike and the mushroom, from the Character Area on the left, onto your new Beach Night page on the right.

4 Drag the mushroom across again, so you copy two mushrooms to level 2.

5 Tap the Beach Night page in the Pages Area on the right. Drag one of the mushrooms on the Stage, so it sits slightly to the left of the other one. If they're too far apart, the game will be too hard or impossible.

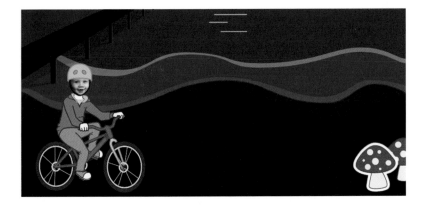

6 Tap a mushroom in the Character Area and drag the **block to increase size** out of its script. Repeat to remove the block from the other mushroom too.

Hot tip

When you're playing in full screen mode, the arrow buttons in the bottom left and right move between pages.

Hot tip

If you drag a block out of a script, any blocks joined on the right go with it. You can drag these extra blocks back into the script.

163

Beware

Each page has its own green flag script that starts when you tap the green flag if it's the current page, or when you jump to the page using a red block. Make sure you tap level 1 in the Pages Area before tapping the green flag to play again. Otherwise the green flag restarts the crash page.

Hot tip

If you're not sure which mushroom is which, tap one in the Character Area and see which is highlighted on the Stage.

7. We need to make the game go from level 1 to level 2 when level 1 is complete. Tap the Beach Sunset scene in the Pages Area and tap the mushroom in the Character Area. At the end of its script, add a red block to go to page 3. This will move us to level 2 after level 1's three mushrooms have all gone across the screen and the player has completed this level.

8. We need to add a broadcast to tell all the characters when the game is completed. Tap the Beach Night scene in the Pages Area. Then tap the right-most mushroom in the Character Area and add a broadcast block to the end of its script. This sends the "orange" message when the last mushroom finishes crossing the screen.

Don't forget

Because we added it as the third page, level 2 is actually on page 3 so the red block has a 3 on it. Page 2 is our crash sequence. We added the pages in this order so we could complete the scripts for the first level, including crashing, before copying them for the next level.

9. Still on the Beach Night scene, tap the cyclist in the Character Area and give it this script. Tap the box under the speech bubble block and add the message "I made it!".

10. Still on the Beach Night scene, tap the + button in the Character Area and add a house. Drag the house on the Stage so it's just below the sea line, and as far right as it will go, half on and half off the Stage.

11. When the game ends, the house rolls into view from the right, as if the cyclist has arrived home. Add the scripts below to your house sprite.

Below: The game completion sequence.

12 Five shorties

Scratch Cat Maestro

This program composes random tunes and jingles for you. Rather than simply playing random notes, it creates a short sequence of notes in the same key (so they sound good together), and repeats the sequence so it feels like the tune has some structure. Add this script to the cat sprite, on any background.

Hot tip

The scale list contains the notes C, D, E, G and A. After playing the list, the script plays a long C note, which gives the tune a sense of finality.

Don't forget

In Scratch 1.4, the **item random of [list name]** block is called **item any of [list name]**. There is no **set rotation style** block in Scratch 1.4. See Chapter One for the alternative.

Hot tip

Experiment! You can try using different or more notes by changing the scale list. You can incorporate the composed music in your games using the "play music" script and the contents of the notes and scale lists.

1 Click the **Data** or **Variables** button and make variables for all sprites called *counter* and *note*. Make two lists called *notes* and *scale*, again for all sprites.

2 Add the script below to your sprite. This is the one that composes the music. You'll need to create a new broadcast for "set up notes".

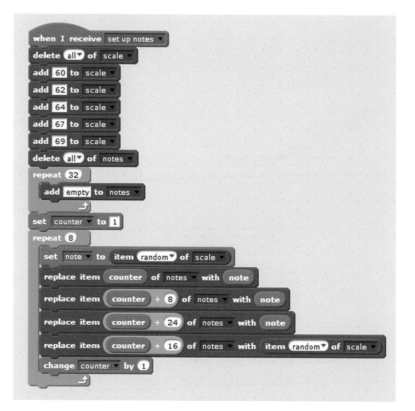

3 Click the **Sounds** tab and use the **Import** or small speaker button to add the "finger snap" sound to your sprite. It's in the Human section of the sounds library.

4 Add the following scripts to your sprite. You'll need to create a new broadcast for "play music". The green flag script composes and then performs a new song when you click the **green flag**. The "play music" script performs the tune. If Scratch composes something you like, you can click this script to hear it again.

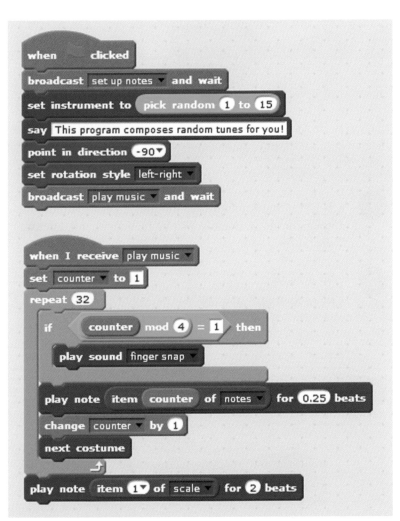

Hot tip

In the "play music" script, try replacing the number 32 with 16, 8 or 4 for a shorter jingle.

Beware

The timing is a bit different on the Raspberry Pi. To keep the finger snap in sync with the tune, move the first **play note** line of blocks to the top position in the **repeat 32** bracket, above the **if** block. If you're using a Model B+, remove the **play sound** block.

Beware

If you click the green flag, your tune will be replaced with a new piece of music.

167

Going Dotty

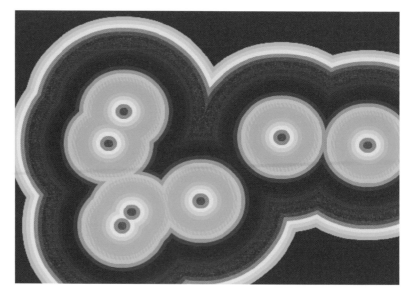

Hot tip

Try swapping the value in the **set pen color** block to the *abs size* variable, to get colors like those shown here.

Hot tip

In Scratch 2.0, try running it in Turbo Mode! You can find it in the Edit menu.

Hot tip

Experiment to make new patterns. Here's one I made in Scratch 2.0 by setting the cat's size and color effect to *abs size* and stamping it, instead of using dots.

This project brings some dotty abstract artwork to your computer. In Scratch 2.0, this program can animate endless patterns. The Raspberry Pi Model B+ is slow with large pens, so the Pi version shows one pattern and pauses before drawing the next one.

Start a new Scratch project and follow these steps:

1 Click the Stage icon beside the Sprite List and click the **Backgrounds** or **Backdrops** tab. In Scratch 1.4, click the **Edit** button.

2 Fill the background with a bright, solid color and click **OK** in Scratch 1.4. Click the **Paint** button (which is a paintbrush icon above the small background images in Scratch 2.0). Add a new background of solid color. Repeat until you have six backgrounds in different colors.

3 Click the **Scripts** tab and add this script to the Stage. You'll need to create the random background message.

4 Make these variables for all sprites: *abs size, counter, how many dots, size*. Create three lists called *colors, x positions* and *y positions*. Clear all the boxes beside them in the Blocks Palette to clear them from the Stage.

5 Click the cat in the Sprite List and add the script below. If you're on a Raspberry Pi B+, change the **repeat 50** to **repeat 25** and insert a **wait 5 secs** block above the **clear** block inside the last bracket.

Hot tip

The **abs of size** operator block here is the sqrt of 9 block with a different option selected in its menu. It takes a number and removes the negative sign from it, if there is one, making it an absolute (positive) number.

Hot tip

For a single dot pattern, take out the **clear** block, change the **repeat 50** to **repeat 25** and change the **set how many dots** block to set the value to 1. On the Pi, remove the **wait 5 secs** block too.

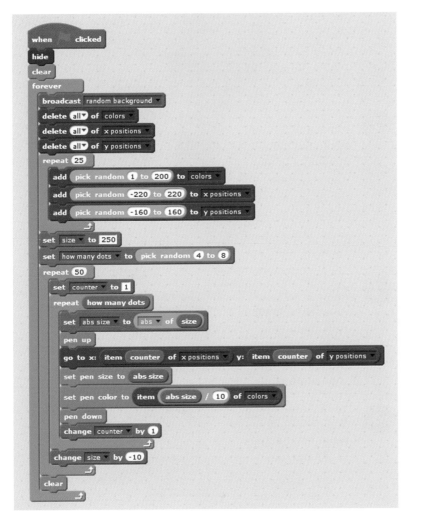

169

Pipeline Defender

In Pipeline Defender, you have to defend the city's oil pipeline from an asteroid attack. Use the arrow keys to move your interceptor to safely destroy the asteroids. If you miss, they will break through the city's defenses until they destroy the pipeline at the bottom of the screen.

Hot tip

This game has lots of potential for you to build on. There's no sound effect, explosion animation or completion sequence, for example.

Don't forget

There is no **set rotation style** block in Scratch 1.4. See Chapter One.

Hot tip

I drew my asteroid by starting with a spot of the largest pen size, and cutting the edges with the Eraser. I copied the "normal" costume to make the "fire" one.

1 Delete the cat. For the interceptor, add the sprite button2 (in Scratch 2.0) or button (in Scratch 1.4).

2 Paint a new sprite for the asteroid. Give it two costumes: one dark, and one red. Rename the costumes to "normal" and "fire".

3 Make a new variable for *score*. Add the first script on this page (above, right) to your **asteroid**.

4 Add the second script on this page to the **button**.

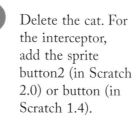

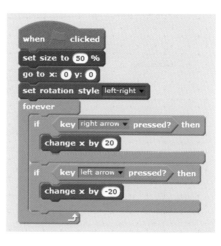

5 Make a variable called *building height* and add this script to your **asteroid**. Click the green flag to draw the skyline.

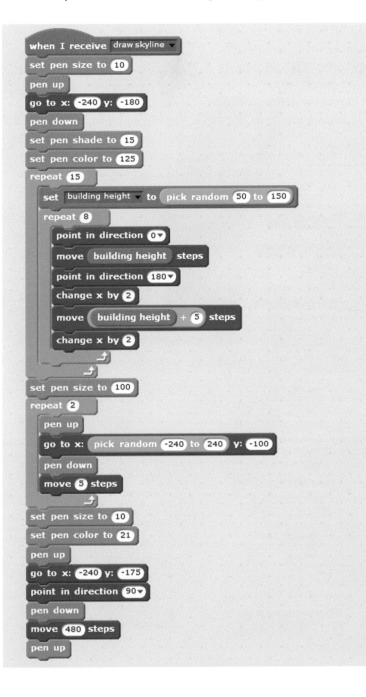

Hot tip

The skyline is randomly generated. First the script draws the skyscrapers, and then two round spots are added to give the landscape a sci-fi feel. Finally, the brown pipeline is laid at the bottom of the Stage.

Hot tip

You can leave the score variable showing on the Stage for this project but you should hide the building height variable.

Hot tip

The pipeline can withstand a mild scorching, but the game's over if it takes a direct hit. When the game begins, check where your lowest towers are. This is where your risk is greatest.

...cont'd

Hot tip

For the dark blue color in the **touching color** blocks, pick it from the skyline. The brown color is from the pipe at the bottom of the Stage. For the **set pen color** block, use the color of the sky on the Stage.

Hot tip

The "Button2" sprite will be called "Sprite1" in Scratch 1.4.

Hot tip

If it's too fast, add a **wait 0.02 secs** block under the **change y by -12** block.

6 Edit the background to fill it with a solid light blue color for the sky. You can't add any stars or other details, because that'll look odd when the asteroid erases bits of them with the chunks of the buildings it strikes.

7 Add the script below to your asteroid sprite. Pay careful attention to the brackets. There's a **forever** block. Inside that is a **repeat 10** block. Inside that is a **repeat until** block and three **if** blocks. You might find it easiest to add these blocks first. In the **repeat until**, add the blocks in this order: **or, or** (in the left hole of the first **or** block), then the three **touching** blocks.

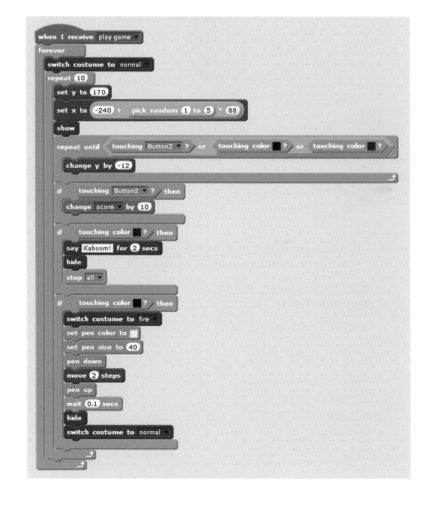

Digital Scoreboard

In Space Mine 3D, you saw how to make digital number costumes for a sprite. In this project, you'll reuse the number template to make a giant scoreboard.

1   Make a sprite that has costumes for the numbers 0, 1, 2, 3, 4, 5, 6, 7, 8, 9 in that order. See "Drawing the numbers" and "Adding the numbers" in Space Mine 3D in Chapter Six.

2   Make variables for *counter*, *inner count* and *score* (if necessary).

3   Add both scripts on this page and click the green flag to see your score gradually appear, from right to left.

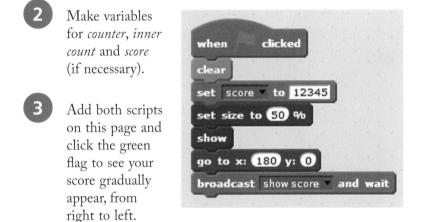

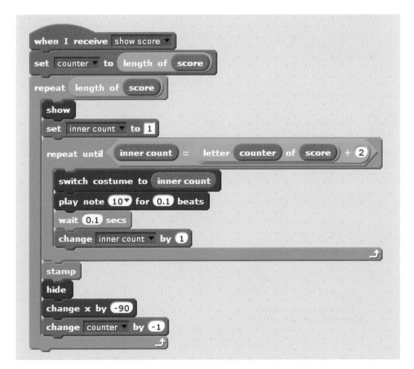

Hot tip

You can save time by starting with your Space Mine 3D project. Keep the red numbers sprite but delete its scripts and all the other sprites. Use the extra eight costume as a template for making all the other numbers. You can change the order of costumes by dragging them in the Costumes Area.

173

Beware

At the time of writing, there is a bug on the Raspberry Pi that stops this working fully.

Below: A black background really shows off the numbers.

Baby, I'm a starfish!

Let's finish with a quick ScratchJr game. In it, you tap the starfish to move it up the screen, dodging the other fish.

 Add an underwater background and two fishes, the crab, and the starfish characters. Delete the cat character.

 Position the four sprites as shown below:

To turn the grid on or off tap the **grid** button above the Stage. Use the **full screen** button next to it to play the game.

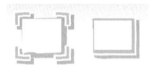

174

 Give the sprites the scripts shown below:

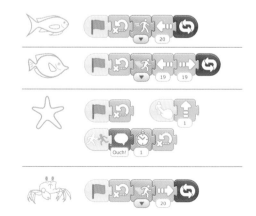

Beware

The starfish has two rows of scripts here. The other sprites all have just one row of blocks.

S